SUCKER PUNCHED
IN THE
FAITH

FIGHTING BATTLES I DIDN'T CHOOSE,
FINDING FAITH I DIDN'T EXPECT

JAYTHAN A SPARKS

SUCKER PUNCHED IN THE FAITH

Fighting Battles I Didn't Choose, Finding

Faith I Didn't Expect

Jaythan A Sparks

Sucker Punched in the Faith
Fighting Battles I Didn't Choose, Finding Faith I Didn't Expect

Published by **Eye Through Faith Publishing LLC**
Still Standing Press Imprint

This book is a work of nonfiction. Names, places, and identifying details may have been changed in some instances to protect the privacy of individuals.

Faith Disclaimer

The reflections on faith, spirituality, and belief expressed in this book are personal and experiential. They are not intended to prescribe doctrine, replace pastoral counsel, or serve as theological instruction. Readers are encouraged to interpret the material through their own beliefs, traditions, and understanding.

ISBN: 979-8-9943196-0-4

Printed in the United States of America

TABLE OF CONTENTS

DEDICATION

To my mom

The first voice I ever knew.

The first prayer that ever covered me.

The first love that never wavered.

You gave me more than life. You gave me a name, not just any name. Jaythan. You created it because you wanted something different. Something that would make people pause and say, "Wait… I haven't heard that before." And you were right. On September 28, 1962, I was the first. No one had carried it. Not in our family, not at school, not in the phone book. Just me. Your Jaythan.

And then… There was JayDee.

That name, the one only you could say just right, wrapped around me like a blanket on cold nights. Doesn't matter if I was five or fifty when you said "JayDee." Everything else faded. The world got quiet. I felt safe. Loved. Known.

Looking back, I realize something: you've always seen me as more than I was. Not just your son, but someone marked. Someone with a purpose, even when I couldn't see it myself.

And honestly? I wouldn't be here to write this if it weren't for you.

I mean that literally.

When I came into the world, I wasn't breathing. Blue. Still. The doctors were moving fast. What about you? You were already on your knees in spirit, if not in body, praying like only a mother can. And then... a cry. A gasp. Life.

You didn't just give birth to me. You fought for me.

And it wasn't the last time.

That fever, the one that made my body burn like it was trying to escape itself, you stayed awake. Doctors dunked me in ice water, but you stayed present. Fear must've been screaming in your chest, but you didn't let it win. You held onto faith like a lifeline, like it was the only thing keeping me tethered.

And then, at three years old, there was a seizure in the car.

I don't remember it. But I've heard the story so many times it lives in my bones.

You pulled over. No panic. Just a purpose. And when instinct wasn't enough, you did what no handbook told you: you put your keys in my mouth to keep me from choking. A mother's quick mind. A mother's fierce love.

You stood in the gap when I couldn't stand at all.

And here's the thing, I didn't know any of this until years later. By then, I had words for faith, for prayer, for miracles. But back then? I had none of that.

But you did.

You believed in God for me before I could think for myself. Your faith wasn't loud. It wasn't performative. It was steady like a heartbeat beneath everything.

And that quiet, relentless trust became the foundation of my own.

I didn't first learn about God from a pulpit. I knew it from you. From your hands clasped in the dark. From your voice whispering prayers over my bed. From the way you refused to let go of me, of hope, of God.

So yeah… this book? It's yours.

Not just in name, but in spirit.

Because every word I wrote, every truth I uncovered, every moment I kept going when I wanted to quit, it echoes back to you. To your courage. To your love. To the woman who stood first… so I could stand at all.

Mom, I'm still here.

Breathing.

Writing.

Living.

JayDee.

And I always will be because you made sure of it.

ACKNOWLEDGMENTS

You know, I'm not sure this book would even exist if it weren't for one person: my wife, Baybee. I mean, seriously, from the very first shaky sentence to the final edit at 2 a.m., she never once doubted I could do it, even when I did, especially when I did. There were nights I wanted to quit. Days I stared at the screen like it had personally offended me.

And every single time, she'd... show up. Not with some grand speech, but with a non-assuming tone, a quiet "You got this," or a prayer whispered so softly I almost didn't hear it, but felt it.

She kept telling me this story mattered. That it could help people, that it wasn't just my story; it belonged to others, too. And honestly? I didn't always believe her. But I believed in her. And that was enough to keep going. So yeah. This book? It's ours.

And I'll never be able to thank her enough, but I'll continue striving to. To my mom - wow. Where do I even start? Your faith didn't just raise me. It held me. Through every twist, every silence, every moment I didn't know which way to turn, I'd hear your voice. Singing. Praying and reminding me that God's still on the throne, even when the floor feels like it's giving way. You taught me to trust not just in Him, but in the process. In the promise. You believed someone would one day play your piano... and here I am, fingers on the keys, heart full of your songs.

You're my foundation. My first prayer. My constant. And no matter how old I get, I'll always be your JayDee. Dad... I wish you were here. But your voice? It never left. It's in the quiet moments. In the advice I find myself repeating, sometimes word for word, like I've got this little speaker in my chest playing back your wisdom. That one thing you said, "Take care of your mom," man. That wasn't just a request. It was a mission. A compass. A promise I carry with me every single day.

This book? It's for you, too. Every page. Every word. I wrote it with your strength in my bones. To my grandparents. Both sides, thank you for the invisible threads you wove into my life. The proverbs you'd drop like seeds: "God doesn't lead you somewhere He won't provide." The way Grandma pointed to the sky and said, "See that blanket? That's God tucking us in." The way Grandpa would nod, hands folded, and say, "Wait on God." You didn't just raise me. You shaped me.

Your faith wasn't loud; it was steady. And that's the kind that lasts. I still see you in the way I think, the way I pray, the way I hope. And I hope I'm making you proud.

Little BIG brother - man, we've been through it, haven't we? Growing up, we learned the hard way how fast things can go sideways. But you? You were always right there. Not saying much and just being there. You helped me navigate the streets, literally, yes, but also the ones inside my head. The ones where doubt lives.

Where fear tries to take over. And even though you're younger, you became my protector in ways I never expected. We didn't need words. Just presence. And that bond? That loyalty?

I carry it with me like armor. My oldest brother, remember those records you left behind? I used to sneak into your room, put on your vinyl records, and listen for hours. That's where I learned about rhythm, soul, and storytelling. Those albums? They were my classroom. And "Boxley," yeah, that silly nickname you and your boys came up with, I know it was a joke. But it made me feel like I belonged.

Like I was part of something. At a time when I really needed that. So thanks. For the music. For the name. For the path you paved. And my sister, my only sister, you've been a rock. I always thought I was protecting you, walking ahead and watching your back. But the truth is, you protected me too, with your strength, your faith, your relentless belief in me. You've been one of my biggest cheerleaders, even when I couldn't cheer for myself. And I don't say it enough, but I see you.

I honor you. And I'd walk through fire for you again in a heartbeat. Mr. Sidney J. Bruce, I still think about the first time you sat beside me at that piano. You didn't just teach me notes. You taught me meaning. You showed me that music isn't just sound, it's feeling. It's memory. It's healing. It's dreaming You unlocked something in me that day.

And every time I play, I hear your voice: "Now listen to what the keys are saying." You're gone, but your influence? It's in every chord. And finally to you. Yes, you, holding this book in your hands. Thank you for walking with me through the pain, the questions, the moments I wasn't sure I'd make it. Thank you for trusting me with your time, your heart, and your own story. My hope? That somewhere in these pages, you see a little bit of yourself. That you feel seen. That you remember, no matter what you've been through, you're still standing and still fighting. Still here.

And that means something. Because after all the sucker punches life can throw? We can get back up. We do get back up. And sometimes we even learn how to dance again. Thank you.

FOREWORD

Sucker Punched in the Faith is a courageous and heartfelt journey through some of life's most difficult challenges and moments of uncertainty. Jaythan invites us into his world with writing that is both deeply reflective and honest. His candid storytelling pulls you alongside him, allowing you to experience the depth of his emotions and the strength it takes to keep moving forward.

What makes this book so compelling is the way it offers a new perspective, a clearer understanding of what faith truly is, what it looks like in real time, and the everyday ways we are reminded to lean on it. Whether or not you have faced the same trials he has endured, you will undoubtedly recognize pieces of your own journey within these chapters.

As you read, consider the challenges you have survived, the obstacles you have overcome, and the moments when faith, whether understood or unnamed, carried you through. You made it. You're still here. And this book is a powerful reminder that being beat up by life does not mean we have to remain broken by it.

Gwyn Burnett

PROLOGUE

The Night I Almost Let Go

I was alone in my room again. Just me, the dim glow of the monitor, and the soft, steady hum of the dialysis machine, my nightly companion for years now. The tubes ran like quiet rivers from my body to the machine and back, doing what my kidneys couldn't. I barely noticed the cold touch of the lines anymore. It was all routine, like brushing my teeth. Like saying a prayer, I wasn't sure if it was being heard.

But that night... something felt different. It wasn't just my body that was hooked up.

It was my soul. I lay there, staring at the ceiling, watching the shadows shift like old memories playing on a cracked projector. The last five years kept flashing through my mind the accidents I somehow walked away from, the music I poured my heart into, the dreams I chased like they were leading me somewhere sacred. And through it all, I thought I had this faith thing figured out. Solid. Unshakable.

But now? Now I was tired. Not just "need-a-nap" tired. The kind of tired that sinks into your bones, your breath, your prayers. The kind that makes you wonder if God's even in the room anymore.

And here's the thing, I didn't stop believing He was real. That wasn't the problem. It was the silence. The feeling that I'd been doing everything "right," walking the line, trusting the process, and still got sucker punched in the middle of the journey. You don't expect faith to hurt like that. You think it's supposed to protect you. Shield you. Keep the worst from happening. But I learned the hard way:

Faith doesn't stop the punch. It's what's left after the punch. It's the whisper in your chest when you're flat on your back, lights blurring above you, wondering if you've got one more try in you. This book? It's not a sermon. I'm not standing on a stage with a Bible in one hand and answers in the other.

This isn't about religion, not about rituals, church rules, or who's doing what on Sunday morning. And it's definitely not one of those "Three Steps to a Better Life" guides. (Spoiler: I don't have three steps. I've got scars.) No, this is just my story, the messy parts. The moments I raised my hands and thanked God, as if He'd moved mountains. And the ones I curled up and whispered, "Why even bother?"

It's the story of a ten-year-old kid, barefoot, dusty from summer in La Puente, who looked up at a hill and saw a cross. Just a simple wooden cross, really. Nothing fancy. But something about it stuck like it was meant for me.

And it's the story of the man who, from a kid, became a man who lived long enough to find out that faith isn't simple at all. That isn't very easy. Painful. Beautiful. And sometimes, barely holding on. So if you've ever felt like you were the only one going through it… If you've sat in a quiet room and wondered, "Is anyone even listening?" If your faith has ever been knocked so flat you weren't sure it'd get back up… Then maybe just maybe this story will remind you that you're not alone. That someone else has stared at that same ceiling. Felt that same ache. Asked those same questions.

And still got back up. But before we get to that night, the machine, the silence, the weight of it all, we have to go back. Back to that dusty California summer. Back to a boy who didn't know his life was about to be marked by a cross on a hill… And a God who wasn't done with him yet.

PREFACE

"This is the story of getting sucker punched over and over and somehow, still finding the strength to get back up."

Yeah. That line? It's not poetic. It's not polished. It's just... true.

I started writing this book in 2017. I remember that year like it was etched into my bones. At that time, I was on dialysis seven days a week, ten hours at a stretch, connected to a machine that performed the work my kidneys no longer could. It drained me completely. Not just physically, though the exhaustion was undeniable, but emotionally and spiritually as well. There were mornings I'd wake up and lie there, wondering if I had the energy to face another day of needles, restrictions, and that constant hum of the machine like a soundtrack to survival.

But still, I wrote.

Not fast. Not smooth. Some days, it was just a sentence. Other days, a paragraph I'd scrap by morning. But I kept going because even then, in the thick of it, I knew this wasn't just my story. It belonged to someone else, too. Maybe someone is sitting in a clinic right now, staring at the ceiling, wondering if they'll make it. Perhaps someone is tired of pretending they're okay.

I wrote because I needed to believe it mattered.

Then, on August 31, 2020, everything changed.

A kidney. A transplant. A second chance so real it still feels surreal.

I don't have the words for the gratitude that flooded me that day. Not really. How do you thank someone, a donor, a stranger, a miracle in human form, for giving you life? How do you wrap your head around carrying someone else's organ inside you, knowing their loss became your breath?

And here's what no one really tells you: healing isn't the end of the fight. It's the beginning of a new one.

Suddenly, it wasn't just about surviving; it was about protecting survival, daily meds. Endless appointments. Blood tests that could turn your world upside down with one number. You learn to live in a state of quiet vigilance. You flinch at a cough. You hesitate before hugging someone. You Google symptoms at 2 a.m. like it's a hobby.

And then came the pandemic.

If you're immunosuppressed, "stay safe" isn't advice; it's a lifeline. Every headline felt like a threat. Every sneeze in the grocery store had me scanning the room like I was in a spy movie. I won't lie, there were times I wondered if I'd traded one prison for another.

There were scares, too. Rejection markers are creeping up. Lab results that made my stomach drop. Nights when I prayed so hard my jaw ached, begging God to hold me together just a little longer.

But, and this is important, there were also wins.

Like waking up one morning and realizing I hadn't thought about being sick. Just... got out of bed. Made iced tea. Felt normal

Or the first time I walked through a park and didn't count the minutes until I needed to sit down.

Or the day I laughed so hard I forgot to be careful.

Those moments? They weren't flashy. No fireworks. But they meant everything.

Because genuine faith isn't about never falling. It's about getting up again. And again. And again.

Now, here we are at the end of 2025. And this book? It's finally done.

Eight years. Not because I couldn't write. But because I wasn't ready to tell the whole story. Not until I'd lived the following chapters. Not until I'd survived dialysis, the transplant, the pandemic, the fear, the doubt, the quiet miracles in between.

This isn't just a memoir. It's a testimony.

And the testimony isn't that God kept the punches from landing because He didn't. Life still came at me like a heavyweight with bad intentions.

No, the testimony is that I kept getting back up. That every time I was knocked down, something more profound than willpower pulled me to my feet. Something that felt like grace. Like presence. Like a whisper saying, "Not today."

I'm not the same man who sat down to write in 2017. I'm not even the same man who walked out of that hospital in 2020.

I'm someone else now.

Stronger? Maybe. But more scarred. More aware. More grateful for small things like a whole night's sleep, or a walk without fatigue, or the simple act of breathing without thinking about it.

To be alive. To be writing. To be standing here, it's not luck. It's not just medicine.

It's renewed faith.
It's a stubborn hope.
It's grace that refuses to let go.

And if my story can remind even one person that they're not alone, that the blows don't get the final word, then every painful, beautiful step of this journey was worth it.

CHAPTER 1

A Cross on the Hill

Back in the early seventies, my favorite summers were the ones I spent at my grandparents' place in La Puente. That house… man, it wasn't just a house. Not to me. It felt more like a whole little world, alive with people, noise, and love.

The front door was always open. Like literally, never locked. Windows cracked just enough to let that hot California air drift through. The garage door is up half the time, so anyone could walk in and say, "Hey."

And somebody always was. An uncle under a car, covered in grease, cussing at the engine like it owed him money. An aunt on the phone, laughing so loud you'd hear her three rooms away. Cousins running in and out, tracking dirt on the floor, not even apologizing because they knew they were welcome.

But right in the middle of all that? Mother.

That's what I called her. Not Grandma. Mother. I don't know how it started, but that's what everyone in the family said, and for me, it stuck. Sounded deeper than "Grandma." Felt warmer. Like she wasn't just family, she was home.

She always smelled like honey, cinnamon. flour, sugar, and butter are melting in the pan. She was always in the kitchen, making something. Cookies one day, cake the next, pie crusts rolled out slow and careful, like it mattered. And whatever came out of that oven? You could taste the love in it.

Every time I got ready to leave, she'd hand me a paper bag, stuffed full. "Love-sack," she called it. I used to think that was funny. Didn't get it then. But now I do. It wasn't about the food. It was her way of saying, "You're loved. Don't forget that."

Papa wasn't around much during the day. He worked long hours at one of my dad's gas stations over in L.A. Sixty miles away, that's a haul, especially back then. But sometimes, if I were lucky, he'd let me ride with him. Man, those days meant something.

I'd wipe windshields, pump gas, and hand folks their change. Nothing big. But it made me feel useful. Grown. And the way those men talked? Car talk mixed with politics, like fixing a carburetor and voting for Nixon, was part of the same conversation. I didn't understand most of it, but I listened. You learn more that way.

Most days, though, I stayed behind with Mother. And when I did, the whole neighborhood was mine. I'd ride my bike down to the corner store for a candy bar, or climb the rocky side of that little mountain near the back of her house. Sometimes I'd sit on the swings at the elementary school. Empty in the summer. Hot sun beating down. Just me and the silence.

But Mother had a way of keeping me in check without ever raising her voice. All she had to do was tilt her head, look at me sideways, and say, "Jaythan, don't give 'em your slapping hand."

I used to nod like I knew what she meant. Truth is, I had no idea. Not then. But over the years, it sank in. She wasn't just talking about hitting someone. She was telling me not to hand my power over to anger. Not to let frustration make me small. That phrase stayed with me. I've said it to myself more times than I can count.

And every morning, like clockwork, she had one ritual. The Price Is Right. She'd sit in her chair, coffee in hand, eyes locked on the TV, yelling at Bob Barker like he could actually hear her. "Five hundred dollars! Come on, Bob, that's way too low!" I'd laugh, but part of me loved it. Seeing her that excited, that alive. It made me happy to watch her be happy.

You know, I think about those mornings now and wonder if she really thought he could hear her? Probably not. But it didn't matter. It was her moment. Her joy. And she took it.

In a life full of hard things, she taught me that joy doesn't have to be big to be real.

The Spirit of Adventure

When I got restless, I would walk out the door all the time. Didn't need a plan. Didn't even put on shoes half the time. I'd start off singing some tune I made up, kicking at rocks, letting my feet decide where to go.

Didn't matter. The neighborhood knew me. I was The Sparks' grandson. That was enough.

That's how I found the hill. Not because I was looking for it. Just wandered my way there one morning, following this narrow dirt road that curved up behind the houses. The higher I went, the quieter everything got, as if the world were holding its breath.

The noise from home, cousins yelling, radios playing old Motown, cars honking down the street faded. Then there was nothing but wind and birds and my own footsteps.

And then... I saw it.

At the very top, standing alone, was a wooden cross.

Old. Weathered. Paint peeling blue and white, barely hanging on. The wood was cracked, leaning a little to the side, like it had been through storms and still stood. To me, it looked huge. Ten feet tall if it were an inch. Maybe more. Felt like it was touching the sky.

I stopped walking. Just froze.

I swear I'd passed that spot dozens of times. But I never saw it, not until that morning.

Funny how that happens. Something can be right in front of you your whole life and still show up for the first time when you're ready.

Sunlight cut across it in patches, like God was spotlighting it just for me. And get this, I don't know why, but I didn't feel like I was looking at it.

I felt like it was looking back.

I sat down beside it, right on the hard ground. Didn't care about the dirt. Looked up and started talking to God. Not like in church. Not formal. Just me, whispering like He was right there, like we were having a conversation.

My prayers were simple. Kid stuff. "God, I want a bike for my birthday." "Can I go to Disneyland this year?" That kind of thing.

But to me? They weren't small. They were everything.

Sometimes I'd cry. Didn't know why. Just felt something profound, something I couldn't name. Other times, I'd talk out loud like another boy was sitting next to me, nodding along and making sense of the world together.

In those moments, the world felt both too big and just right.

And that cross? It wasn't just wood stuck in the dirt. It was more than that. A doorway. A marker. A sign that said, without words, You're not alone.

I didn't have the language for it then. Didn't call it holy or sacred or spiritual. But I knew it meant something.

Even as a ten-year-old, I could feel it, this quiet pull toward something bigger than me.

Something that knew my name before I did.

Curiosity and Consequences

I was curious. Maybe too curious.

And when you're a kid, curiosity doesn't always stop at "what if." Sometimes it runs straight into "let me try."

One summer day, back at home, that part of me almost got me killed.

I found a bullet. A .38 caliber. Just lying there. Don't even remember why. But seeing it, holding it, something about it felt dangerous. And that made it enjoyable.

In my head, I thought, what if I could make it pop like a firecracker?   Not a big explosion. Just a spark. A flash. Something to see.

So, I got this idea, pull out the gunpowder, light it, watch it burn fast and bright. Seemed simple enough. At least, it did in my ten-year-old brain.

I grabbed a hammer. Found a nail. Placed the tip against the base of the bullet, like I was trying to open it. Then I hit it.

The second the hammer struck, boom.

It wasn't loud enough to be a gunshot. More like a sharp crack, like a tree limb snapping under pressure. But the pain?

That came fast. Red hot. Centered in my thumb.

I looked down and blood everywhere. Pouring. It had its own mind. And the tip of my thumb? Gone. Just... missing. Flesh peeled back, bone maybe showing. I don't know. I couldn't focus.

I stood there, frozen. Not screaming and not crying. Just staring.

Then panic hit.

But here's the thing, my first thought wasn't about dying. It wasn't about the pain. It was, I'm gonna get in so much trouble.

Like that mattered more.

My parents must've heard the noise or seen me run in. Next thing I knew, they were rushing me to the ER. I remember their faces tight. Scared. Trying not to show it, but I saw it anyway.

Lying on that hospital table, lights too bright, voices around me talking fast, "nerve damage," "lucky he didn't lose more," "could've been his eye," I started shaking.

Not from cold. From realization.

This wasn't a game anymore.

That one choice, just a few seconds of "what if," could've cost me everything. My hand. My life. Could've left my family to pick up the pieces.

And for what? A spark?

I walked away with a scar. Still have it. Look at it every time I sit at the keyboard or piano. But I also walked away with something more profound.

A sense that life is thin. Fragile. Like glass.

Even as a boy, I knew then you don't need a big moment to change your whole story. Sometimes all it takes is a hammer, a nail, and one bad idea on a quiet afternoon.

You make one move. One split-second decision.

And nothing's ever the same.

Music Awakening

Not long after that summer with the cross on the hill, something else started growing inside me. Music.

I don't exactly know when it began. Maybe it was always there. But that's when I first noticed it, like a quiet hum beneath everything else.

In our house, music wasn't just playing. It was living with us. Like air. Like light. You couldn't escape it, and honestly, nobody wanted to.

My mother would put on gospel records early in the morning, songs so full of power they'd pull you out of bed whether you felt like moving or not. Mahalia Jackson. The Hawkins Family. James Cleveland. That kind of sound. Deep. Holy. Unapologetic.

My father? He liked his jazz and blues. Smooth stuff. Late-night kind of music. Miles Davis. John Coltrane. B.B. King. Otis Redding. Muddy Waters. He'd sit in his chair, eyes closed, head nodding slowly, like he was listening to secrets.

And my oldest brother, man, he kept that turntable spinning. R&B all day. The Delfonics. The Spinners. Marvin Gaye. Stevie Wonder. Whatever was hot, he had it played loud first. Made the walls shake.

Me? I was taking classical piano lessons at the time. So during practice, it was Chopin, Bach. Beethoven. Scales. Arpeggios. All that discipline.

But the minute I walked out of my piano lesson? That's when the real music took over.

The kitchen was gospel. The living room was blue. The hallway was R&B. And somewhere in between all of it, I started finding my own sound.

I didn't know it then, but I wasn't just learning notes. I was learning how music could carry feeling. How could it tell a story without words? How it could open a door inside you that nothing else could reach.

Music became my safe place. A way to breathe when things got heavy. A way to connect to something bigger than myself, even if I didn't have a name for it yet.

Back then, I wouldn't have called it purpose. Or passion. I just knew one thing: when I played, I smiled. When I played, I forgot about everything else. It was like dreaming.

And the beauty was in the mix.

The Gospel taught me to look up. Taught me faith had a sound.

Blues taught me to feel. Taught me pain could sing.

Jazz taught me to bend the rules. To make something new out of what was already there.

R&B taught me groove. Taught me rhythm wasn't just in the beat, it was in the way you moved through life.

And classical? That gave me discipline. Showed me that greatness doesn't come fast. It comes with time. With work.

Each one planted a seed. I didn't see it then, but later, every single one came up in the music I made. In the path I walked.

Looking back, I can see how that cross on the hill and the music in our house were doing the same thing, building a foundation under my feet before I even knew I needed one.

One rooted me in where I came from. The other gave me a way forward.

I didn't know both were about to be tested. Hard. In ways I never saw coming.

Eventually, my love for music found its way into church.

By then, I was already studying piano with Mr. Sidney J. Bruce, a rigorous but intentional teacher. Every note mattered. Every finger placement. He didn't smile much, but I respected him. He showed me that music wasn't just talent, it was a craft.

But I wanted more. I wanted to play gospel the way I heard it with fire, with freedom, with hands that knew how to shout.

So I started taking lessons from the church pianist, too. Learned those rich chords. Those runs. That way of playing where your hands seem to dance ahead of your mind.

Within months, I was playing for the youth choir.

The first time I sat at that piano in front of people, my hands wouldn't stop shaking. Keys felt slick. My heart was pounding like it wanted out.

But then someone nodded. Someone smiled. And something clicked.

Like I belonged.

The older folks would say, "That boy's got something special." Part of me loved hearing that. Who wouldn't?

But it was more than pride. It was deeper. It was like… I had a reason to be there. A place to put all that restlessness. All those questions, I didn't know how to ask.

And yes, there she was.

The pastor's daughter.

She noticed me. Not just my playing. Me.

And I noticed her. Maybe she liked the way I played. Perhaps she just wanted the attention. Or maybe, just maybe, we were both young and figuring things out.

Either way, it felt like the world was opening up. Like doors were cracking open, I didn't even know they existed.

Sundays Were Non-Negotiable

Sundays were different. Not just another day. They had their own rhythm, their own rules. My mother didn't ask us to go to church. She expected it every week. No debate. Saturday nights meant ironing clothes, laying them out neatly on the bed, shirts folded just right, shoes shined, socks matched. Everything ready.

Sunday mornings? Chaos. My siblings and I racing to the bathroom, pushing each other aside, trying to get to the sink first. Breakfast was quick, maybe toast, juice, something light, then we'd all pile into that yellow-and-green 1968 Chrysler 300. Man, that car was nice. Only 10 years old, and we were proud of it.

And every time I opened that door to get in, I'd remember I used to fight my mom about this. Hard.

This was way before I started playing piano at church. Back then, I didn't want Sunday mornings. I wanted afternoons. I enjoyed the park. I wanted to play baseball with my friend Vincent. (I'll tell you more about him later; he mattered.)

But my mom? She wasn't moving. "No baseball on Sundays," she said. That was the end of the conversation.

Even if I had my glove in hand, already halfway out the door, I'd try one last time. Remembering what the coach said the day before that games would be every Sunday. My heart sank before I even asked.

I'd look at her. She wouldn't even turn around.

"You're going to church," she'd say. "End of discussion."

As if we'd ever discussed it at all.

The ride to church had its own soundtrack. Literally.

Donny Hathaway on the 8-track. "Put Your Hand in the Hand." That song would come on, and something in me would shift. The music wasn't just playing; it was pulling me somewhere. Making me feel alive before we even pulled up to that little storefront on 53rd Street: Gethsemane Christian Love Baptist Church.

And every Sunday, we'd walk in and there it was, my mom's painting on the wall.

God's hand reaching down from a cloud. Big. Bold. Real. And under it, those words: "If the Lord be God, follow Him. But if Baal, then follow him." From First Kings. Chapter 18, verse 21.

That was her work. The pastor had asked her to do it because everyone knew my mom could draw like no one else. Not just pretty pictures. She could make faith visible.

But her creativity wasn't just in paint. It was in the way she prayed. The way she sang. The way she raised us. Looking back, I see it now, my own way with music, the way I write, the way I play, even how I feel a song before I finish it, that came from her.

I didn't know it then.

For years, I didn't even understand what that verse meant. To me, it was just words under a painting I loved because my mom made it.

But later, after the cross on the hill, after the dialysis nights, after the transplant, after everything, I remembered it again.

And something clicked.

It wasn't just a Bible quote. It was a choice. A real one. Who are you going to follow? What are you going to stand on when the ground shakes? What's going to guide you when you can't see the path?

I couldn't explain it at ten. But I felt it.

And deep down, I knew it mattered.

At church, when they called for soloists, my mom would rise.

She didn't hesitate. Didn't check her hair or straighten her dress. Just stood up and sang.

Songs like "If I Perish" are bold, fearless. Or "I've Got a Long Way to Go to Be Like the Lord" honest, humble, full of soul.

Her voice filled that small church. Reached every corner. Shook the walls.

And yeah, sometimes I was embarrassed. Kid stuff. Didn't want my mom to be that loud, that passionate in front of people.

But most of the time? It anchored me.

Like, no matter what else was happening, I was home.

Still, something changed over the years.

I stopped fighting. Stopped counting the Sundays I missed baseball. Stopped wishing I was anywhere else.

Not because someone made me change. Not because the sermons suddenly made sense.

But because I started listening.

Not always to the pastor. Sometimes I zoned out during the message.

But I listened to the music. To the way people clapped. The way faith didn't just sit in pews, it moved, it breathed, it lived in our family like that old 8-track playing Donny Hathaway on repeat.

And slowly, without even realizing it, I stopped resisting.

And started belonging.

Reflection

Looking back now, I can see how all those pieces fit together. Didn't make sense at the time. Not even close. But now?

Now I get it.

My grandmother's steady presence. The front door was always open. The scar on my thumb from that stupid mistake with the bullet. That cross on the hill weathered, leaning, like it had been through storms and stayed standing anyway. My mother's faith is rock solid, no negotiations. And the piano keys under my fingers, sticky from summer heat, waiting for me to find the right note.

They weren't just moments. They were foundation stones.

Laid one by one, long before I knew the storm was coming.

At ten years old, I didn't understand much. I thought faith meant protection. Like if you believed enough, life wouldn't hit you too hard.

But it does. Faith doesn't keep the danger away. It just gives you something to hold onto when you're in the middle of it.

I didn't know then that curiosity could save you and break you at the same time. That stubbornness could keep you going or keep you stuck. That talent? Yeah, it opens doors. But it also brings weight. Expectations. Pressure.

All of it can be a blessing. And all of it can become a burden.

But there was one thing I did know deep in my gut, even as a kid.

Somewhere above me, someone was listening.

Not because I had proof. Not because I felt it every day.

But because sometimes, when I sat by that cross, or played a song that came out better than I planned, or heard my mom pray like she knew the One she was talking to, I'd get this quiet sense.

Like I wasn't alone.

Like I was being held, even when I didn't feel it.

That cross on the hill? It became my first altar.

Not official. Not built of stone. Just wood in the dirt, sun-bleached and cracked.

But it was holy.

The place where I first whispered prayers about bikes and Disneyland. The place where I cried without knowing why. The place where I felt something bigger than me, even if I couldn't name it.

And over the years, I carried it with me.

Not in belief every single day. Some days, there was doubt. Some days, it was anger.

Some days, it was just a memory.

But still I carried it.

Because even when faith feels thin, the shape of it stays.

And that cross? It wasn't just wood.

It was the beginning of a conversation that never really ended.

CHAPTER 2

Sunday Rules & Silent Questions

Like I said before, Sundays weren't up for debate in our house. Not even close.

For my mom, they were sacred. Period. She didn't do options. Didn't believe in them when it came to church. You went. That was the rule. No discussion. No exceptions.

Saturday nights? They had their own rhythm, a ritual.

She'd pull out our clothes, pants creased just right, shirts pressed till they snapped, dresses starched so stiff they stood up on their own. Then she'd get the shoe polish, kneel, and work until every scuff was gone. Shine them up like they mattered. Which, to her, they did.

Then she'd set everything by the door. Ready. Waiting. Like Sunday wasn't just coming, it had already arrived.

Sunday morning would hit, and the house would turn into a battlefield.

My siblings and I running full speed down the hallway, elbows out, trying to beat each other to the bathroom. "I was here first!" "You took forever yesterday!" "Mom, he's hogging the sink!"

And she'd yell from the kitchen, voice cutting through the noise like a whistle, "Y'all better hurry up! God don't wait on nobody, and neither do I."

Man, that line sticks with me to this day.

I'd roll my eyes, mumble something under my breath, pretend I didn't care. But deep down? I wanted to be anywhere else.

I wanted to stay home. Wanted to go to the park. Wanted to play baseball with Vincent.

Or sit with my dad and watch TV, lazy and slow, no shoes on, no rules.

But that wasn't how it worked.

Sunday mornings belonged to God. And to Gethsemane Christian Love Baptist Church on 53rd Street.

At least, that's how my mom saw it. And in our house, how she saw it, that's how it was.

Funny thing is, I didn't hate church. Not really.

I hated the idea of having no choice. I hated feeling like my time wasn't mine. But even then, I couldn't explain why those mornings stuck with me.

The music. The way people sang like they meant it. The way my mom's voice rose without fear. The painting on the wall is hers, with the verse from First Kings: "If the Lord be God, follow Him."

I didn't understand it all. Not then.

But I felt it.

And over time, something shifted.

I stopped fighting. Stopped wishing I was somewhere else. Started noticing things.

Like how the piano made my chest vibrate when someone played just right. Like how silence could feel holy if everyone was actually listening.

Like how a sermon could land not because it was loud, but because it touched something real.

And slowly, without even realizing it, I began to show up differently.

Not just my body. My heart too.

But still, there were questions. Quiet ones. The kind you don't say out loud.

Why does it have to be this way?

What if I don't feel what everyone else seems to feel? Is faith supposed to feel this heavy?

I didn't have answers. Not yet.

But I kept going.

Because even when I didn't understand, I knew one thing: I was being shaped.

And I didn't know it then, but those Sunday mornings? They weren't just about rules.

They were building something in me. Something I'd need later. When the real tests came.

The Ride

We'd pile into that car, man, it was huge. Like, super big. One of those old school models that took up two parking spots and made noise just sitting still. You could see it coming from down the block.

Mom is behind the wheel. We kids crammed in the back, pushing each other, laughing, sometimes fighting over who got the middle spot. And gospel music? Always playing. Loud.

Came through the speakers like it had something to say. Sometimes the radio, sometimes the 8-track. Donny Hathaway. The Hawkins Family. James Cleveland. Songs with names we didn't always know, lyrics we didn't fully understand.

But here's the thing, I didn't need to understand them to feel them.

Even then, I could tell this wasn't just music. It was carrying something. Something deep. Like it was speaking to parts of me I hadn't even discovered yet.

And it sank in. Slow. Quiet. But sure.

By the time we pulled up to that little storefront church on 53rd Street, I was usually half-awake. Still groggy. My mind drifts, dreaming about the baseball diamond near our house. I imagine myself at bat, the crowd cheering, the ball cracking off the bat, that kind of dream.

But the second we walked through those doors?

Everything changed.

It wasn't just the noise. Or the heat. Or the smell of perfume mixed with floor wax.

It was the weight of the place.

Like the air itself was different. Thicker. Fuller. Like something invisible was moving in the room.

No more daydreams. No more wishing I was somewhere else. Even my body seemed to know this wasn't just another building.

This was sacred.

And I didn't have the words for it then. Didn't call it holy. Didn't label it spiritual.

But I felt it.

And that feeling? It stayed.

Longer than the songs. Longer than the sermons. Longer than I ever expected.

The Atmosphere of Church

Gethsemane wasn't a big cathedral. It wasn't some grand church with stained glass and echoes. Just a storefront, really. Small. Humble. We had folding chairs, a few wooden pews, and fans handed out with funeral home ads on the back. Nothing fancy.

But it didn't need to be big. The sound filled every corner.

The choir sang like they were trying to break through something, as if they sang loud enough, heaven would answer. And the pastor Reverend Charlie Jackson, at the time, preached with fire. Pastor L.C. Jackson would replace him a few years later. He was younger. Sharp dressed. Drove a Corvette.

To me, that made him the coolest preacher alive. I remember thinking, A man of God can drive something like that? Made faith feel real. Not stiff.

The adults all came in their Sunday best. Clothes pressed, shoes shone, hats just right. The older saints prayed out loud, calling things down like they knew God was listening closely. Others stayed quiet, heads bowed, lips moving but no sound coming out.

I watched them both. Tried to figure out who God heard more, the ones shouting or the ones whispering.

And then there were us kids. We'd nudge each other. Whisper jokes. Laugh when the ushers weren't looking. Act like we weren't paying attention.

But we really were.

Somehow, in between the poking and the giggles, the music and the words still got through.

Silent Questions

Even as a boy, I had questions I didn't know how to ask out loud.

Why did my dad stay home while we went to church? He wasn't against faith. He'd been raised in it, too. But he didn't come. I thought about it a lot. Never asked him why. Maybe I was afraid of the answer.

Why did God sometimes feel close and other times so far away? When I sat by that cross on the hill in La Puente, it felt like He was right there. But when I prayed for a chance to play baseball and received no answer, I wondered if He even heard me.

Why did faith sometimes feel more like rules than a relationship? Don't do this. Don't go there. Don't question that. I wanted it to feel like freedom. But too often, it just felt like fences.

I kept those questions inside. Tucked them behind the polite smile I wore on Sundays.

The Missed Baseball

Baseball was my quiet way of pushing back. I wanted to play so bad I could taste it. I'd practice with Vincent, the friend I mentioned earlier, tossing the ball back and forth in the tight space between our houses. He was fast. Confident. The kind of kid who just looked right at a field. When he made the park team, I wanted in.

I still remember the ache in my chest when the coach said, "Games are on Sundays." Vincent would try to get me to skip church. I always told him no. That wasn't an option. But after I said it, my mind would drift while sitting in church, listening to the choir, trying not to think about baseball.

At the time, it felt unfair. Later, I saw it differently. But back then, it was just another reason to wonder if faith is about God. Or about church? Or rules that make kids like me miss out?

Faith in Action

Still, faith had a way of slipping in the back door when I wasn't looking.

I remember my little brother and me talking one afternoon after being at church all day. We were whispering. "Why do we have to go anyway?" he asked. I always said, "To help us be better kids." I think he felt the same way I did. Like building faith was starting to feel like a chore. It was getting heavier each week.

I usually found comfort in those moments when I'd hear my mother singing in the kitchen. Songs like "Through It All" and "Pass Me Not." Her voice was firm. Steady. Even when money was tight or life felt hard. I didn't always believe the words myself, but hearing her sing them made me believe in her faith.

And here we were, my little brother, complaining about church like it was the problem. But back then, I had no idea how much my mom was carrying. Her struggle didn't even cross my mind.

Reflection

Looking back, I realize those questions I kept inside were part of my faith journey too. They started small, in silence, without answers. But they mattered.

In Chapter 1 of my book, I found the cross on the hill. In Chapter 2, I faced the rules, the quiet moments, and the things I couldn't understand. Together, they laid the foundation for what would later become a struggle between belief and doubt, between following rules and having a real connection.

I didn't know it then, but the questions I carried would prove just as crucial as the answers.

CHAPTER 3

Music as Escape, Music as Calling

M usic had always been around me. But it wasn't until church pulled me in that I started to see how much of myself was in it. At first, it was just part of Sunday, the choir, the songs, the organist playing chords that made the room feel alive. But over time, music became more than background noise. It became a place to hide. A lifeline. A way to feel bigger than the life I was stuck in.

The First Notes

The piano sat in our living room like it belonged. It wasn't tucked away. Wasn't covered in dust or mail. It was right there, polished, ready, like it had always been meant to be in the center of our home. My mother made sure of that.

She had promised herself as a little girl she'd always have a piano in her house, no matter what. And she kept that promise. Sometimes I think she wanted me to play before I even started. She'd tell me how her father sold her childhood piano, how it broke her heart, and how she swore music would live in her home again. When I touched the keys for the first time, she looked at me like she already knew, like she'd been waiting for me to carry it forward.

At first, it was work. Real work. My first teacher, Mr. Bruce, had sharp ears and sharper eyes. He taught me on Saturday mornings. More than once, he could tell when I hadn't practiced when I was guessing, faking my way through the notes. "Jaythan," he'd say, tapping his finger on the music stand, "you can't halfway play. Either you know it, or you go home and practice until you do."

I'd roll my eyes when he wasn't looking, but I listened. At home, I'd practice. Over and over. My fingers stumbled across the black and white keys until they started moving on their own. Some days, I got so frustrated I'd slam the lid shut and walk away, angry. But a few minutes later, I'd come back, sit down again, determined to get it right. I just hoped my mom didn't hear me slam the piano lid.

Then it happened the first time my hands played with absolute freedom. Clear. Strong. True. It wasn't just noise. It felt like something bloomed in the room. Something bigger than me. I sat there, stunned, realizing I had made that sound.

After Seeing the Potential

When my parents saw that I really liked the piano, that I genuinely wanted to learn as much as I could, and especially after my music teacher, Mr. Johnny Spencer, from my Henry Clay Jr. High School days, encouraged them, they enrolled me in the Eubanks Conservatory of Music. Looking back, I'm proud to say I actually met Mrs. Eubanks, the founder and director. She listened to me play, checked my skill level, and signed me up for my first jazz piano and gospel organ classes. That was an exciting time for me.

After training there, I won a place in the Who's Who in Music award. As a young boy, still in grade school, getting an award like that made me feel like I was on top of the world. I was so grateful then. I still am. Mrs. Eubanks gave me guidance and training that stayed with me. Later on, it helped me get accepted into the New England Conservatory of Music in Hartford, Connecticut.

Playing for the Choir

The first time I played for the youth choir, I thought my legs would give out. My palms were sweating so much that I had to wipe them on my pants before touching the keys. I remember sneaking a look at the front row. My grandmother was watching me, her eyes locked on mine, lips pressed together in that half-smile that said, Don't you dare quit now.

The director counted us in. The choir started singing. I put my fingers down. The notes weren't perfect. I stumbled once or twice. Hit a wrong chord. But no one stopped. They kept going. So I kept going. And somewhere in the middle of it, I stopped worrying about the mistakes. I just let the music carry me.

When the song ended, I wasn't that nervous boy in the corner anymore. I was part of something. People clapped. Patted me on the back. A couple of girls said, "You played well!" during service. I shrugged like it didn't matter. But inside, I was shining. Excited. Proud.

Mr. Bruce wasn't interested in me playing gospel piano. Or any style besides classical. He called it Western European soul music. At the time, I called it boring. It made me feel confined. Restricted. That was because I wanted to play how I felt. Playing music exactly as it was written, the same way every time, the way it had been done hundreds of years ago, felt dull to me. To my mind. My soul. My spirit. But I still respected Mr. Bruce very much.

Music Instead of Baseball

Music became my way out when church life got hard. When I couldn't play baseball on Sundays because the games were at the same time, I'd go to the piano. It filled that space. When I wanted to sleep in or stay home and watch Westerns with my dad but couldn't, the piano made it easier to let go.

It was what I turned to when the rules felt too heavy. Too unfair. I couldn't change my mom's mind when she said "No" about baseball. But I could sit down and play. I could put my hands on the keys and let the frustration out. The music never told me "No." It always made room for me.

Mistakes and Lessons

Of course, not every Sunday was a victory. I still remember a concert I played for the choir, The Voices of Watts. In the middle of a song, I completely lost my place. My fingers froze. The choir turned their heads. The director gave me that wide-eyed look, like, "Sparks, you better play something." My heart pounded, and for a split second, I thought about getting up and walking away.

But I didn't. I just started hitting chords, fumbling through until somehow it started sounding right again. By the time the song ended, I was sweating more than Robert the director, but nobody laughed, nobody scolded me. In fact, an older gentleman pulled me aside and said, "Son, that's how you learn. You mess up, you keep going. That's life."

That stuck with me. Not just for music. But for faith. For living.

A Secret Language

The more I played, the more I realized music was a language I could speak when words failed me. I'd always been shy about talking in front of people. I'd stumble over my words. Sometimes, my little BIG brother, Chris, would step in and say what I was trying to say when I got stuck. But at the piano, there was no stutter. No pause. The music came out clear and strong. And people listened.

That gave me the confidence I never had before. I didn't always feel like I belonged. But when I played, I felt needed.

Reflection

Looking back, I can see it clearly. Faith was my foundation. But music became my anchor. When doubt came, when questions about God's silence started to whisper at me, I could always go back to the piano.

It didn't matter if it was a whole church or just a quiet afternoon at home. The music held me steady. It reminded me I wasn't just a boy asking questions into the dark. I was a boy with something to give. Something that could carry me past those questions.

Music was an escape. Music was calling. Music was survival.

And in many ways, it still is.

CHAPTER 4

The Neighborhood Boys

A few of the boys in my neighborhood were my first real tribe outside of family. They weren't saints. But they weren't thugs either. Just boys. Funny. Loud. Competitive. Always looking for something to do.

One of my closest friends, the one I mentioned before, was a kid named Vincent. He was short, stocky, quick on his feet, with a grin that could get him out of trouble before it even started.

I first met him outside our houses. We lived two doors down from each other. He was throwing a baseball against the wall of his house, catching it clean, like he'd done a thousand times. I asked if I could join. Without hesitation, he said, "Sure." That was all it took. We were friends from that moment.

We spent hours in the narrow space between our houses, tossing the ball back and forth, talking about everything and nothing. Besides my grandfather and uncle, Vincent was the one who really pulled me into baseball. He was always at the park, always on the field. One day, he brought me along. Watching him hit, run, and throw it made me want to be part of that world. It wasn't just a game. It was a way to belong.

Not all the kids around were like Vincent. Some were older. Harder. Already leaning toward gangs. Guys from other blocks would come to the edge of our street, trying to pull us in. One day, three of them cornered me by the side of my house. "You gonna roll with us or not?" one said, trying to sound tough.

I was scared. Before I could answer, my mom's voice cut through the air: "Jaythan! Get in here, it's time to practice piano before dinner."

I ran inside. Saved by music again.

Years later, I told my little brother about that moment. But back then, I kept it to myself. Swallowed the fear. Never spoke of it.

Looking back, it must have been meant for my mom to have me practice so much. For one, it kept me away from the wrong crowd. And then it gave me a chance to be on television.

Yes, as a little kid, I was on TV with my cousin. I wrote a song on the piano, and he sang it. We auditioned. We passed. They taped the show. But before it aired, it got canceled.

After that, another opportunity came up, Chuck Barris' The Gong Show. We made it through the audition, but we were too serious for the actual show. It was silly. Clownish. More about making people laugh than real talent. I'm kind of glad we didn't get on.

But one thing's clear, music kept me out of trouble. It protected me, even in my own neighborhood. It saved me from that group of guys, more than once.

The Soundtrack Interrupted

For all the baseball. For all the talk about gangs. The real disruption came on an ordinary day in 1975.

My little brother and I were outside, he riding isbig-wheel, and me on skates bouncing a basketball in front of our house, right there on the corner. The summer air was heavy but nice, the kind of day when kids would play until the streetlights come on. We were laughing. No worries at all. Then it happened.

I heard it before I saw it, the crash of metal hitting metal, a car slamming into another down the block. I turned my head just in time to see one of those old heavy cars coming straight at us.

"Get out of the way!" I shouted at my little brother, my voice cracking. He swerved off and got clear. I didn't.

There was no time to move. No time to think. The car hit me. Next thing I knew, I was under it, rolling across the concrete, my head smashing into the edge of our flowerbed border. Pain shot through me, sharp, blinding. For a second, all I saw was white. Then everything went dark.

Hospital Days

When I woke up, I was in the hospital. The smell hit me first: antiseptic, sharp, cold. It wasn't home. It scared me. I didn't know if I was broken for good.

My parents were there. I can still see their faces. My mom's eyes are full of tears. My dad is trying to stay strong, but he's shaking, like he's seen something he can't unsee. They didn't say much at first. Just being there said enough: You're alive. We almost lost you.

The doctors told me I had a concussion. My body was bruised and banged up, but I'd made it through. Something that could've gone the other way didn't.

Funny thing, the hospital started to feel like a second neighborhood. The nurses treated me like I belonged. Gave me extra snacks, teased me when I got quiet, tucked me in at night like I was theirs. One janitor, especially, took a liking to me. He'd push my wheelchair down the hall, racing me while pretending his mop was a horse. It was silly. But it made me laugh. Made me feel like I was still a kid. Like life wasn't over.

The man in the bed next to me turned out to be someone I wouldn't recognize until years later. At the time, he was just a kind older man who told jokes to make me smile. That's all I knew. Later, my mom told me it was Dan Rowan from Laugh-In. Back then, I was thirteen. Didn't care about Hollywood. But as I got older, it hit me that the strange part of it was. I, a boy who thought he might never laugh again, am sharing a room with a man whose whole life was about making people laugh.

The Aftermath

The physical injuries healed faster than the ones you can't see. After I got out of the hospital, the doctors said I should see a psychiatrist and a psychologist. Help me process what happened. At thirteen, I didn't even know what those words meant. All I knew was I had to sit in a chair and answer questions about how I felt.

At first, I didn't want to talk. I was afraid they'd think I was weak. Or worse, crazy. But over time, those sessions taught me something: trauma isn't just in your body. It's in your mind too. And if you don't face it, it stays. Grows.

I remember the psychiatrist asking me that day, "What did you think about when you saw the car coming?"

Without thinking, I said, "My little brother. I wanted to make sure he was safe."

That surprised me. Even as I said it, it showed me that in the middle of fear, my heart still knew how to protect. How to love.

The psychologist told me that instinct wasn't just bravery. It was faith. Faith that someone else mattered more than I.

It felt strange, sitting in those rooms, talking about God with people trained to speak about the brain. But for me, the two were constantly connected. My body survived. But it was my faith that kept me from breaking under the weight of fear.

Reflection

Looking back, that accident was more than just a boy getting hit by a car. It was the first time I realized how fragile life is. And how strong faith can be.

The boys in the neighborhood gave me company. Baseball gave me something to dream about. But the accident gave me a different perspective. I had faced the real chance of not making it at thirteen years old. And I came out still breathing and still believing.

I didn't have the words for it then. Didn't know how to explain what I felt. But I do now. That was the day I started to understand what resilience really means. Not that you aren't afraid. But you keep going anyway. You get back on the skates. You keep walking. You keep believing.

Even at thirteen, I whispered it under my breath: God must really love me.

CHAPTER 5

The Crossroads

Crossroads don't always come with signs or arrows. Sometimes they show up in everyday life. A friend calls you outside when you know you should be practicing. Sunday morning duties pulling one way, Saturday night freedom pulling another. Mine came quietly. Long before I had the words to name what I was feeling.

My friends outside the church were testing limits, sneaking beers, chasing girls, and getting close to trouble. I saw it. I wasn't blind. Part of me liked their boldness. Their laughter. The way they seemed to live without consequences.

But every Sunday morning, I was back at Gethsemane. Fingers on the keys. Deacons nodding. Choir swaying. One deacon pulled me aside once. Said, "Son, God's got His hand on you. Don't waste it."

Those words should've lifted me. But sometimes they felt heavy. Like a leash. What if I wanted to waste it? What if I just wanted to be normal?

The Push and Pull

The school added another layer. I went to Cleaveland High, Locke High, and Verbum Die High School. Some of my peers called me "piano man." Sometimes it was respect. Sometimes it was sarcasm. My friends would push me, say, "Come on, just skip rehearsal, hang with us."

I still remember one Friday afternoon. A high school buddy tried to get me to go to a football game at another school across town. My heart wanted to go. But in my head, I kept hearing my mother's voice: "Remember, integrity is doing the right thing even when no one is looking."

I didn't go that day. Instead, I sat at home. Stared at the piano. Felt angry. Not at my friend. Not even with my mom. Angry at God for making everything feel like a test.

And yet, music saved me. It gave me a shield. A direction. I could say no to things because I had something else pulling me forward. But even music had its moments of doubt. Was it just a way to escape? Or was it something more? A calling?

Early Adult Crossroads

By my late teens and early twenties, the questions got sharper. I wasn't a boy under my mother's roof anymore. I was a man trying to find my own way. And faith in something I had grown up with now had to be chosen.

That was the hard part. Realizing that going to church, playing piano, and even quoting Scripture didn't mean I was believing for myself. Faith felt heavy. Some nights, I lie awake asking, "Is this real for me?" Or is it just what I've always known?

At the same time, music was opening doors. Clubs. Recording sessions. Side gigs. Places that didn't feel like Gethsemane at all. In smoky rooms or late-night rehearsals, I felt free in a way I never did in church. My deep voice. My playing. People respected me there. But even as I thrived, guilt stayed close. Was I turning my back on where I came from? Or was I finally becoming who I was supposed to be?

It felt like I was walking two roads at once. One path was the boy raised in the A.M.E. and Baptist churches, taught discipline, duty, respect. The other was the young man drawn to rhythm, creativity, art, and the unknown. Neither felt wrong. But they didn't seem to meet either.

A Preview of the Struggle to Come

Looking back now, I see the crossroads wasn't one moment. It was a season. A long stretch of learning to live with tension and no clear answer. My mother's prayers, her lessons they kept me grounded. But my own restlessness kept me searching.

That's when faith changed for me. It stopped being about rules. Started being about questions. And once you start asking, the questions don't stop. They multiply.

This part of my life wasn't the hardest, that came later, with bigger crashes, illness, and nights I almost gave up. But this was the setup, the quiet warning. Faith wasn't broken yet. It was being tested. Stretched. Changed.

At the crossroads, I lived in both worlds, the boy from the church. The man is stepping into the city. And though I didn't know it then, God was shaping me. Preparing me for the sucker punches still coming.

Reflection

Crossroads don't go away just because you make a choice. They stay inside you. Remind you that faith isn't a straight line.

Back then, I thought the hard part was choosing between right and wrong. But now I see it wasn't about that at all. The real struggle was learning to trust that God could be with me in both places. In the sanctuary. In the smoky rehearsal rooms. In the rules of the church. In the freedom of music.

A crossroads isn't about finding the perfect answer. It's about learning how to keep moving, even when you feel pulled in two directions. What felt like a fight back then, like a tug-of-war in my chest, was really preparation. Training for the kind of faith I'd need later. When the sucker punches came harder. And faster.

CHAPTER 6

When Faith Felt Heavy

By the time I was in late adolescence, church wasn't just something I went to. It was part of my weekly rhythm. Sundays. Rehearsals. Midweek services. Special programs. Gethsemane Christian Love wasn't just a building. It was the place that shaped how I saw faith and community, how I saw myself.

Reverend Charlie Jackson, the one who baptized me, had a steady presence. His voice made you feel warned and comforted at the same time. After he passed, Pastor L.C. Jackson took over. He was younger. More energetic. Had a flash about him. I'll never forget seeing him pull up in his sports car. To a teenager like me, that was the definition of cool. I felt more connected, like he could reach me where I was.

It was under Pastor Jackson's leadership that I found my place on the piano. I started playing for the youth choir. At first, everything clicked. I wasn't just filling a role. I had a purpose. I had talent. And it mattered. For the first time, I wasn't doing it for free.

That sense of purpose gave me confidence. Playing meant I wasn't invisible. They didn't pay me much, but to me, although it was small, it meant something. It was validation. My faith. My music. My skill. All working together. I thought, This is what it's supposed to feel like.

But harmony doesn't last forever.

Somewhere along the way, tension came in. The same deacons who once supported me began to change. One man in particular, the same one who told me years before, "Son, that's how you learn. You mess up, you keep going. That's life." He wanted me to keep playing. But suddenly, didn't want to keep paying. "You should do it as a service," he said. "You should do it for God."

His words carried weight not just because he was older. But because he framed it like a spiritual duty. If I pushed back, it didn't feel like I was saying no to him. It felt like I was saying no to God.

That's where the cracks started.

I began to see the politics inside the church.

It wasn't about the money itself. It was what the money represented. It told me my time, my gift, my effort had value. When they took that away, it wasn't just losing a few dollars. It was losing recognition. It was watching people, even church people, twist faith to fit their convenience. I was young, but it left a mark.

I started noticing other things, too. Arguments behind closed doors. Petty jealousies dressed up as "concern." Power struggles that had nothing to do with God but everything to do with control. I began to understand that the church, as holy as it felt on Sundays, was still made of people. And people carry their flaws wherever they go.

There were nights after service when I couldn't sleep. I'd think about it. Remember my mother's songs. Her voice rose in the kitchen when I was a boy. Back then, faith felt pure. Safe. Now it felt heavy. Was it supposed to be this hard? Was it normal to feel crushed by the very thing that was supposed to lift you?

And yet, even when the weight pressed down, something else stayed alive.

Every time I sat at the piano, I felt release. The music reminded me that faith wasn't about pleasing people. Or winning approval. It was about connection. When my fingers hit the keys, I felt like I was talking to God past the noise, past the rules, past the expectations.

That's the strange thing about faith: it can hurt and heal at the same time.

Looking back, I see how those years at Gethsemane shaped me. They taught me faith isn't always light. Sometimes it's tangled in human pride, disappointment, or obligation. But they also taught me resilience. How to tell the voice of God apart from the voices of men.

Even now, when I think about those Sundays on 53rd Street before the church moved to 96th, I can still see myself at the piano, caught between joy and frustration: worship and weariness.

That tension followed me into adulthood. Not just about church. About faith itself.

While learning, I realized faith isn't just about lifting your hands in praise. Sometimes, faith is carrying the weight and choosing not to put it down even when it feels heavy.

Reflection

Faith was never meant to be confused with people. But when you're young, they blend. I didn't know then that the church could be both a sanctuary and a battleground. That the same voices lifting you could also hurt you.

What I carried from that time wasn't bitterness. It was the beginning of discernment. I learned that genuine faith isn't about applause. Or paychecks. Or whether the deacons approve. Authentic faith is choosing to keep showing up.

Keep playing. Keep believing even when it's heavy, even when you're tired.

Those years taught me something I still hold onto: faith doesn't make life easier. But it makes you stronger under the weight.

CHAPTER 7

The Wreck and the Take Off

The day of the second crash is etched in me in a way I still can't fully explain. I was thirty years old on my way to a recording session in Long Beach. It was supposed to be a typical day. Music. Soundboards. Maybe some laughs in the studio, nothing out of the ordinary.

I stopped at a fast-food place. They didn't have what I wanted. No big deal, I thought. I'll go to the next one. That small choice, something I didn't even think about, changed everything.

Back in the SUV, I did something I still see in my mind: I didn't buckle my seatbelt. "It's only a mile or two," I told myself. "No need." Just like that. Casual. Reckless. But accidents don't care how far you're going. They happen in seconds.

I was driving about forty-five miles per hour when I saw a young woman pushing a stroller across the street. My eyes followed her to make sure she was clear before I passed. Then, in that exact moment, I heard a sound sharp, metallic, like something breaking in a dark alley. A car spun into oncoming traffic. Into my lane. Coming right at me.

Time slowed.

I thought of the young woman, I thought of the baby in the stroller. If I swerved toward them, I could have killed them, no question. So I held the wheel, and under my breath, I said, "Oh God."

Then, the impact of metal hitting metal, and Glass shattering. My body was thrown forward. Then silence. Violent silence.

When I opened my eyes, there was a woman who had been on the other side of the street. Leaning over me. Voice soft but urgent. "Are you ok? Is there anyone I should call?"

I could feel blood running down my face. My eye. My cheek and chin. I told her to call my mom.

She didn't have a pen, so she took my parents' number and wrote it on her arm with the blood that was running down my face from the cuts and bruises.

I found out later her name was Felicia Crumbly, to whom I'll be forever thankful.

I learned that when my parents got to the hospital, the staff told them the man from the other car had been brought in lifeless. For a moment, they thought it was me. My mom wouldn't accept it. She shook her head. Said, "No. That's not my son." I could imagine that my mom's mind went back to 1975 when she saw me laying underneath that car wedged in our flowerbed. Faith does strange things in the middle of horror. That day, she reached into the chaos and pulled me back.

The Aftermath

The doctors listed the damage: left orbital bone fracture, punctured cheek, sprained wrist, bruised ribs, and injured hip. One of them said something I'll never forget. He told me that if I had been wearing a seatbelt, the force of the crash, with me going forty-five mph, and the other driver, sixty mph or more, might have killed me. My size, nearly three hundred pounds at the time, had felt like an anchor, keeping me in place and alive.

What I thought was a weakness had become my shield.

But the injury that stayed with me wasn't the broken bones or the bruises. It was my left eye.

One surgeon walked into my room, holding charts. Eyes tired. "There's about a forty percent chance you could lose sight in that eye," he said. His voice was calm, professional. But those words hit hard. Forty percent. A number heavy enough to bend your breath. Then he added, "You've been through something extraordinary. Don't expect your body to snap back."

For days, I couldn't shake it. That number ran through my head. I prayed until my throat hurt. Cried until my pillow was wet. Then prayed again. But the fear didn't leave.

I didn't tell my parents. Too afraid to add that weight to them.

My faith, the one I'd carried since childhood, felt cracked. I started asking questions I never thought I would: Why did this happen? Hadn't I done good things? Hadn't I stayed on the right path? Hadn't I served?

I used to think faith was a formula: do right, live clean, trust God, and He protects you. But the accident broke that idea. I was learning faith isn't a deal. It's a lifeline. And sometimes that line feels thin. Sometimes it feels more like silence than song.

Therapy and Echoes of the First Crash

The physical injuries were only half the fight. My mind was its own battlefield.

Because I'd hit my head again, the doctors suggested I see a psychiatrist. Again.

He asked me to describe the crash. I started talking. My voice broke. My hands shook. "I heard the sound first. Then I saw the car. Then I thought of my brother."

"Your brother?" he said, tilting his head.

And suddenly, it came. I wasn't just talking about the crash at thirty. I was back at thirteen. Back in front of my house. On skates. Bouncing my basketball. The first accident. The car is spinning toward me. I screamed my brother's name before it hit.

The room spun. I hadn't thought about that moment in years. But now, the two crashes were on top of each other like two films playing at once.

The psychiatrist said, quietly and softly, "Your body remembers, even when your mind tries to move on."

That stayed with me. Not just then. Still does.

Trauma isn't just something you remember. It's something your body holds. Waits. Carries until the right moment or the wrong one brings it back.

Cracks in Faith

One night, lying in bed with my left eye throbbing, I started bargaining with God. If you heal my eye, I'll be grateful forever. If I can see clearly again, without problems, I'll never complain again.

But in the middle of that prayer, something hit me: God wasn't negotiating. He wasn't weighing my good deeds against my bad ones like it was a trade. Faith wasn't about leverage. It wasn't about earning. It was about trust, even when there was no deal to make.

That didn't come like lightning. It came slowly. Painful. Like giving up something I didn't want to let go of.

Some nights, I still felt angry. Betrayed. Other nights, I held on to just a little hope. But the cracks in my faith? They let in light I hadn't seen before.

Preparing for Japan

Weeks turned into months. My body healed enough that I could move without constant pain. My left eye, though scarred, kept its sight. The doctors said it was remarkable. But I knew the truth: my mom's prayers, my own tears, and something greater had carried me through.

It was during this fragile time, still recovering, that another door opened: an opportunity in Japan. At first, I almost laughed. Japan? Me? Now?

I wasn't going for music at first. The contract was for audio engineering, sound system setup, and installations. Safe work. Technical. No spotlight. But deep down, I felt it was more than that. A new chapter. Maybe even a fresh start.

I thought back to the two crashes: the boy at thirteen, the man at thirty. Both times, metal twisted. Bones broke. Faith shook. And both times, I walked away. Scarred. Shaken. But alive.

Maybe Japan wasn't random. Perhaps it was the next part of the story God had been writing all along.

Reflection

The wreck nearly took my eye. Nearly took my life. Nearly took my faith. But it also gave me some perspective. It forced me into silence. Into therapy. Into hard talks with doctors who made me face the weight of trauma I'd carried since I was thirteen.

And it set the stage for takeoff. Literally. Spiritually.

I didn't know then what Japan would bring. Didn't know how it would test me. Change me. Reshape what I thought about music. About who I was, about faith. All I knew was this: I had survived two crashes. And maybe, just maybe, God was getting me ready to fly.

CHAPTER 8

Off to Japan

The shift came in the form of an unexpected opportunity: Japan.

For a young man from Central Los Angeles, the idea of traveling halfway around the world felt unreal. I had grown up with gospel records playing in the house, jazz and blues on the radio, soul music in my bones, and the grit of the city all around me. That was my world. Then, suddenly, I was getting ready to leave it all behind to go somewhere where the language, culture, and rhythm of life were completely different. The thought excited me and scared me.

I wasn't going for music at first. I had a contract as an audio engineer. My job was to install sound systems and set up treatments in different venues. That was the plan. That was the role. But life has a way of breaking open what you think your purpose is.

The more time I spent in those spaces, the more they asked me to do. Sound engineering. Then DJing. Then, before I knew it, I was back on stage as a musician and even as music director. Not because I planned it. Because they needed it. And because I could do it.

It started with my voice. Deep. Strong. Clear. They said it carried well in a room. That voice got me on the mic doing voiceovers, playing CDs, and making audio & video recordings. Then one day, someone asked me to play piano. Just a few chords. Then a whole song. Then another.

My contract had become something else. Something I didn't see coming.

I started in Nagoya City, setting up soundboards, stacking speakers, and doing the technical work. But the journey took me to Yokohama, then Osaka and many other cities, and finally back to Nagoya. Each town had its own feel. Its own pace. In each one, I was stretched. Changed. Learning not just new skills, but new ways to trust.

And through it all, I realized something: faith doesn't just go with you. It grows when you do.

The First Night

My very first night in Japan, I didn't get a chance to breathe. Right from the airport, bags still in hand, I was taken straight to work. The rehearsal hall felt like another world. I couldn't understand most of what people were saying. We used hand signals to communicate. I got through the night, but when I finally walked into my hotel room, exhaustion hit me. And reality.

I stepped out onto the balcony. Looked up at the sky. Whispered to myself: "My mom sees this same sky."

That thought broke me open. The distance. The culture shock. The weight of being halfway across the world from everything I knew all came down at once. I sat there, staring at the moon, and cried. Not because I regretted coming. But because I suddenly realized how much of home I had carried with me. My mother's lessons. My father's quiet strength. The songs she sang while cooking were all inside me.

That night was one of the hardest I'd ever lived through. But her voice in my head stayed with me. Telling me to stand firm. To trust. To be strong in faith. Resilient in spirit.

Staff Who Became Family
Over time, the staff stopped being just coworkers. They became family.
There was Floyd, a sound tech built like a wiry tree branch, thin, quick on his feet, always grinning. His English was broken, my Japanese worse, but we made it work. He'd hand me a cable with a nod. I'd point to a speaker. We'd both laugh when it actually worked. One night after a show, he came up beside me with a steaming bowl of ramen.

"Energy," he said, tapping his chest. That was his way of saying, You belong here.

Then there was Mikki, the floor manager. Sharp. Precise. Always three steps ahead. But off the clock, he loved to tease me. My chopstick skills were terrible. I always bowed too low. He'd roll his eyes, say, "Too much," and pull me back up, laughing. One night, he looked at me and said, "Your voice is big. Not just an engineer. Heart voice." I didn't know what to say. But inside, I knew he was right.

I grew close to Hirono, too, the Boss. Quiet man. When he spoke, you listened. He'd tell me to "tune the frequencies of the room with the speakers, calculate the crowd, balance the sound." Not just technical. He understood that music wasn't only about noise. It was about intention. His calm steadied me.

And then there was Yuromi, the youngest. She followed me around, watching how I mixed, how I moved through a set, how I read the room. After a while, she started calling me "Big Brother Bishop." One night, after a show, she said, "I didn't think... a Black man from America... would teach me. But you do. You give me hope." Her words hit me hard. I wasn't trying to teach anyone. I was doing my job. But for her, my being there meant something. That music could cross oceans. That a voice could matter, no matter where it came from.

And in the middle of all this was Michael. Not staff. Not a musician. Different. We became close friends. He was tied into the Japanese underworld, the Yakuza. Tiptoed, but people respected him. Didn't talk about God very much. Didn't even appear to believe in God. But still, he looked out for me like I was his younger brother. When trouble came near, he showed up. When someone pushed too hard, he made sure it stopped, never said much. But his presence carried weight.

Life in Nagoya, Yokohama, and Osaka

Each city taught me something different.

In Nagoya, life moved more slowly. The streets weren't crowded. People nodded politely and kept walking. The food was rich miso-katsu, breaded pork cutlet with dark miso sauce, which was their pride. I must have eaten it twice a week. Back home, I had a habit of diving into every kind of food, but here, meals felt different. Not rushed. They were meant to be taken slowly. I learned patience at the table.

Yokohama was different. More international. Bigger. I'd walk along the harbor. The air smelled like salt and fried noodles from the stalls. On weekends, the city came alive.

Neon lights everywhere. Crowds poured out of karaoke bars. Business people loosened their ties. Laughter filled the streets. That's where I saw how music could bring strangers together fast. Someone would sing off-key, loud and proud, and the whole room would cheer anyway.

Then there was Osaka wild. Loud. Unapologetically alive. Famous for takoyaki, octopus balls, and okonomiyaki, a savory pancake cooked right in front of you. Vendors flipped them on griddles while people pushed through the crowd. The nightlife didn't quit. Bright lights. Fast talk. Nonstop energy. I remember playing a set one night. The room was so packed I couldn't see the back wall. People clapped on the wrong beats, shouted my name, lifted me like I belonged. And for that moment, I did.

Flight to South Korea

One of the strangest lessons about faith didn't come from church. It came from Michael.

I had once told him I was afraid of flying. Every time I got on a plane, I tried to sleep through it. Never worked. My nerves always got in the way. So when I got a contract for a weekend show in South Korea, my stomach was tight.

Michael drove me to the airport that day. On the way, he looked over and said, "Bishop?" That's what they called me in Japan. Not sure why. Maybe because my name was hard to say. Maybe because of how I carried myself. Like there was something more behind my eyes.

Michael had perfect handwriting. Never seen anything like it. The only person who came close was my oldest brother when we were younger. That day, he handed me a small note to carry with me while in another country. He wrote: Be very careful in South Korea. Watch out for street fights. Then, at the bottom, he added: And Bishop, God's got you.

Now here's the thing: Michael didn't believe in God. Called himself an atheist. Said he didn't buy any of it. And he wasn't just some quiet skeptic. He was a Yakuza, the kind of man who lived by loyalty, not scripture; never quoted Bible verses, never talked about faith.

But still, he wrote those words.

And somehow, coming from him, they meant more. If someone like Michael could say it, maybe it was true.

By the time I boarded the plane, the fear wasn't gone. But it had quieted. I felt safe not because I had gotten stronger, but because faith showed up in the last person I'd expect.

Coming Full Circle

By the time I came back to Nagoya, I didn't just have a résumé. I had a second family. People who had carried me in ways I didn't even know I needed. People who looked past language, past skin color, past culture, and saw me.

Japan started as a job. It became something else. A crucible. A place where my faith grew beyond Gethsemane Christian Love, beyond gospel music and Sunday sermons. It became a faith in people. Faith in staying strong when everything's new. Faith in my own voice, not just how it sounded, but how it connected, even when I couldn't speak the same language.

Looking back now, I see Japan wasn't an escape. It was part of the journey. The same God who kept me alive through broken glass and twisted metal was now showing me a different kind of stage, one where survival and music became the same.

Reflection

Japan tested me in ways no church pew or choir stand ever could. It was there, in the noise of neon streets and in the quiet of lonely hotel balconies, that I learned faith doesn't need a pulpit. It can live in shared ramen after a long night. In a young girl calling me "Big Brother." Even in a note from an atheist with perfect handwriting saying, "God's got you."

My faith stopped being about rituals. It became about presence, God showing up in places I didn't expect. In people I wouldn't have looked for.

Looking back, Japan wasn't just another chapter. It was a mirror. It showed me who I was becoming. Who I still had to become. And how far grace can reach, even across oceans.

CHAPTER 9

Coming Home, Facing Loss

Return to a Different Los Angeles

I stepped off the plane in 1995. Four years in Japan are still on me. And walked into a city that felt familiar, but not the same.

The last time I saw Los Angeles up close was 1991, right after the Rodney King beating. The trial hadn't even started when I left for Nagoya. But the city was already tense, as if something was coming.

While I was overseas, setting up and installing sound systems, riding trains, holding my place in neon-lit clubs, L.A. was burning. Riots. Fire. People demanding justice.

Now, in 1995, I was back. And again, the city was caught in a trial. The O.J. Simpson case was everywhere. Billboards. News vans. Every street corner. Neighbors talked about it while watering their grass. Strangers argued in grocery stores. L.A. was stuck in a mix of waiting and worry.

It hit me harder than I thought. I left a city on edge. Came back to another one just as tense. Why was it that no matter how far I went, trouble was always here when I returned?

My faith was already tested, already cracked, shifted under that weight.

Within days of being back, my pager wouldn't stop. My phone rang all day. Gigs. Studio sessions. Out-of-town jobs. People wanted me. Musically, it was a good time. Opportunity was right there, chasing me down streets that still carried fear.

Music and the Hustle

Japan had taught me about structure. About respect for craft. Every soundcheck mattered. Every bow. Every small gesture. I carried that back with me, not just in memory, but in how I moved and worked, like souvenirs tucked in my pocket.

With the money I'd earned overseas and the work waiting when I got home, I finally had a chance to do what I'd been thinking about since Nagoya, opening my own music school. Teaching kids in Japan changed me. I saw their focus. Their joy when they played their first complete song. The way they treated even a simple melody like it meant something. I wanted to bring that to Los Angeles. Give kids here the same shot.

But the difference was clear. In Japan, discipline felt like a tight, tuned string, clean, steady. In America? From what I remembered, it wasn't like that. The kids showed up late. Parents treated lessons like an option. Respect for the music sometimes got lost in everything else.

Still, I was willing to try. Once I started my school, I knew it would be different. There was something freeing about it. Where Japan gave me order, L.A. reminded me of the wildness that built jazz, soul, gospel music born from improvisation, from pain, from freedom.

I learned to hold both. Discipline and freedom. Structure and chaos. Both matter.

Faith in Transition

Spiritually, I was walking on new ground.

Even before Japan, I had stepped away from Gethsemane Christian Love, the church that raised me. When I came back, I didn't go back there. Instead, I followed my dad. He had started attending St. Mark A.M.E. Church, the same one my grandparents took me to during those early summers in La Puente. Now, my dad was going there too.

There was something steady about that. St. Mark wasn't just any church. It was part of my family's story. And now I was grown, sitting in the same pews, my father beside me.

71

He asked me to play for the church. Of course, I said yes. To me, it was an honor. I wore it like a badge. But there was pressure too. People watched me not just for me playing, but because of who I came from. My parents. My grandparents. Their names carried weight. And every Sunday, I took that weight with me.

It rooted me. But it also showed me a truth: church faith and personal faith aren't always the same.

Still, I played. And when I did, I felt my dad's pride.

The Night Everything Changed

May 22nd, 1997.
That date will never leave me.

I had driven seventy-five miles out for a rehearsal and got home late. Exhausted. I told myself I'd go by my parents' house tomorrow. Like I always did. I never let more than a day pass without checking in. But this time, I waited.

Around 11:30 that night, the phone rang. It was my sister. Her voice was urgent. Shaking. "Get over to Momma and Daddy's house. Now."

I jumped in my car. Heart pounding. Drove across the city fast. When I got there, I saw my father on his back. Paramedics are moving around him. Pushing. Shocking. Trying.

We followed the ambulance to the hospital. Hope trailing behind us, thin as a thread.

A doctor pulled my mother and me into a private room. His words are still in me.

"Mr. Sparks is a very sick man," he said.

My chest loosened. Sick meant alive. I let myself believe that he would come back.

Then the doctor looked at me again. Saw the hope on my face. And said, "Mr. Sparks didn't make it."

The words hit like a brick. My knees gave out. I couldn't breathe. It felt like the floor had opened up and dropped me through.

Later, when they let me go in alone, I stood by his bed and prayed like I never had before. I begged God to take me instead. To reverse it. To do anything but this. I asked Him why so many bad people were still here, while my father, a good man, a faithful man, was taken in his sleep.

None of the old answers helped. "God needed him more." "He's not in pain." They meant nothing. Just empty words. They bounced off my grief like paper hitting a wall.

All I could hear was his voice. From the time I was seven, all the way to the night before he died. Every time he saw me, he said it:

"Hey, cat, be sure to take care of your mom."

The Aftermath

For months, everything was fog. I did what I had to do. Went to gigs. Showed up when needed. But the world felt dull. Like the color had been drained out. Faith, already cracked, now felt like a flat tire. Nothing is holding it up.

The only thing that kept me moving was my mother. She had leaned on my father for years. Now she leaned on me. And that became my job. The one my father gave me over and over: Take care of your mom.

Music became my way through. I poured my grief into the keys. Into chords. Into every rehearsal, every studio session. I didn't always believe in what I was playing. But I played anyway. Hoping the notes would carry me where words couldn't go.

I started saying things to myself. Small phrases. "You are a Sparks." "You are the son of a great man." "You come from strong people." Saying them out loud helped. Reminded me his legacy didn't die with him. It lived in me.

The Breaking Point

But grief finds cracks. Always does.

About four months after my dad passed, I was at a COGIC church rehearsing with the choir. I was on autopilot. Still carrying everything. Then, in the middle of rehearsal, the choir director called me out in front of everyone.

"Jaythan!" she shouted.

I looked up. "Huh?"

Her voice came sharp, impatient: "I know you're still dealing with your loss, but it's about time to get back to rehearsing normally."

The room went quiet. My chest tightened. I saw red, or maybe black, I can't remember.

"Excuse me?" I said. Voice low. Shaking.

She repeated it word for word.

I had to walk out. All the way to the parking lot. So I wouldn't explode in front of people. She followed me outside. When she caught up, I told her something she'll never forget. Didn't yell. Didn't cuss. Just made it clear you don't tell me how to grieve my father.

That was the day I decided: no more letting "church people" define my faith. My spiritual process? That's between me and God. Period. Full stop.

It confirmed what I'd been learning my whole life: *"people are people, wherever people are."* Doesn't matter if they're in a pew or on a street corner. They bring their flaws. Their limits. Their lack of understanding.

It was a breaking point. But also a turning point.

I stopped expecting the church to carry my grief. I realized faith wasn't about clichés. It wasn't about looking okay. Faith was about resilience. About showing up for my mom. About hearing my dad's voice, take care of your mom, and living it, one day at a time.

Redefining Identity

Slowly, the fog began to lift.

I kept teaching. Kept playing. Kept building. I leaned into the discipline Japan had given me. The legacy my father left behind. And the faith that, though worn down, wouldn't let go.

I was learning who I was. Not just a musician. Not just a son. Not just someone running a school under other people's expectations. I was a Sparks. The son of a great man. A man who carried the music and the weight of faith, not the kind made of easy answers or empty phrases, but the kind that holds you up when everything in you wants to fall.

Reflection

Coming home wasn't the triumphant return I'd hoped for. I left Los Angeles with questions. I came back to a city just as broken as my faith. Losing my father made the ache worse.

His death taught me something no sermon ever could: grief doesn't follow rules. Faith doesn't take away pain.

But it also showed me this legacy isn't buried with the body. It lives in the people left behind.

My crossroads at that time weren't about choosing music over trouble or church over freedom. They were about one thing, whether to keep standing at all.

And slowly, note by note, breath by breath, I chose to keep standing.

CHAPTER 10

Regaining Ground

A few years after Japan, and after my father's passing, it still felt like I was standing on uneven ground. Grief had knocked the wind out of me. But music was always the one steady rhythm pulling me back to myself.

When I think about coming home to Los Angeles, it is heavy. Tense. The O.J. Simpson trial was everywhere on every screen, in every paper, on every street corner. And under it all, the memory of the Rodney King beating still burned. Those same emotions came back every time I walked into a hard moment like that day at the COGIC church. It felt like I kept stepping into storms that never let up.

My father's death made the storm worse. I hadn't found a way to stand steady since he was gone. Nights were long. I didn't sleep. Days carried a quiet anger I didn't know what to do with.

But one thing I knew for certain was this: if I stayed at the piano, kept my hands on the keys, kept practicing, kept making music, then maybe, just maybe, I could find solid ground again.

That was my goal then, to regain my footing.

Back to the Music – Jazz, Classical, Teaching

A few years after Japan, after my father passed, I started digging deeper into my jazz playing. Not just the licks I used on stage. Real study. Bebop. Hard bop. Ballads. I wanted to understand it all. At the same time, I returned to my first love: classical piano. The scales. The etudes. The long pieces required patience and focus.

That brought me back to Mr. Sidney J. Bruce, my childhood piano teacher. By then, he was known worldwide as a master instructor. I was one of the early students who studied under him. I still remember walking into his home, feeling like that same wide-eyed boy from thirty years before.

He looked at me. Tilted his head. Said in that deep voice of his: "Jaythan, you've been carrying pain in your hands. Play."

I sat down and started a Chopin piece I hadn't played in a while. I got halfway through when he stopped me. "You see? Your fingers are fast, but your heart is hiding. Again. But this time, don't play to impress me. Play to free yourself."

That was the last thing he ever taught me before he passed.

That moment changed something in me. Under his guidance, I wasn't just relearning music. I was retraining my soul. Every note, every arpeggio, peeled back a layer of grief I didn't know how to name. Music became therapy. Not escape. Healing.

At the same time, I began building my own music training programs. Something I had thought about since working in that academy in Japan. I poured myself into designing lessons and structuring classes for kids who reminded me of myself at their age. It gave me purpose. I could help shape their path even while I was still finding my own.

One student, maybe twelve, came in fidgeting, eyes down. Didn't believe he could play. I placed his hands on the keys. Showed him a simple blues progression. Within minutes, his face lit up. That spark in his eyes lit something in me, too.

In teaching him, I was teaching myself: joy was still possible.

Memories of My Father

Grief doesn't leave quietly. It comes back in grocery store aisles. In the middle of studio sessions. In the silence before sleep.

I kept thinking about a conversation I had with my dad years before, after his mother passed. I asked him how he kept going. How could he still move when loss weighed so heavily?

He said, "Cat, I'll go to her grave. I sit there. Bring flowers. Talk to her. You don't stop loving because someone's gone. You love differently."

Back then, I didn't understand. But after he passed, I found myself doing the same thing, driving to the memorial park. Flowers in hand. Sitting by his grave marker. Sometimes I'd talk out loud. Sometimes I'd sit.

The day I said his name out loud, I didn't break down. I knew something had shifted. Healing wasn't about forgetting. It was about learning how to carry grief without collapsing under it.

One afternoon, as I got up to leave, I could almost hear him:

"Take care of your mom, Cat. That's your job."

Those words became my compass. Pointed me forward when I didn't know which way to go.

Faith Without the Church

During this season, my faith began to shift in ways I hadn't expected.

I felt closer to **God**, but further away from the **church**.

Back to the "Aftermath." It wasn't a rebellion. Wasn't anger. It was clarity.

I realized I didn't need the church to confirm my faith. Too many church people said the same things, empty phrases that didn't touch the pain. After my father died, I had no patience for hearing, "If there's anything I can do, just call." None of that eased the ache in my chest.

I started seeing church differently. To me, it became like a hospital. A place you go when something's broken. When your spirit's off, you get help. But eventually, you leave. You go back out and live. You carry your purpose into the world.

I still went sometimes, especially with family. But my real spiritual work happened in private. In prayer at my father's grave. In quiet moments at the piano. In the silence between notes.

Breakthrough on Stage

Still, healing doesn't come straight. It turns when you don't expect it.

I remember playing a concert at the Universal Amphitheatre in L.A. The crowd was enormous. So loud I couldn't hear myself think. The group I was with gave me a solo. I decided to let go. Just play. Improvise.

Somewhere in the middle of it, something broke open inside me. I stopped thinking about notes. About technique. About grief. The music took over. And for the first time since my father died, I felt joy on stage.

When the song ended, the applause was different. Not just loud. Steady. Real. Heartfelt.

In that moment, I knew: I was still standing.

Redefining Identity

To rebuild, I kept saying the same things to myself: "You are a Sparks." "You are the son of a great man." "You come from great people."

At first, they felt forced. Like I was pushing them into my heart before they could settle. But over time, they started to feel true.

They weren't just words. They were reminders. Of the legacy I carried. Of the bloodline I came from. Of the faith that shaped me, even when I walked away from it.

Music was still my foundation. But who I was, my authentic self, wasn't just in the notes I played. It was the strength I kept walking with. In the lessons my father left behind. In the faith that stayed alive even when I thought it was gone.

Reflection

Regaining ground didn't happen all at once. It wasn't one precise moment. Not one big performance. It was slow. Steady. A quiet taking back of who I was through music, through memory, through faith, changing inside me without me even seeing it happen.

By the time I looked up, I realized something: I hadn't just survived two wrecks, or Japan, or losing my father. I was learning how to live again.

And this time, the ground under me wasn't shaky. I was standing on faith.

CHAPTER 11

The Diagnosis

When I started to get my footing back regain my balance, my faith, my sense of who I was the letter came folded twice. White. The kind that looks official before you even open it.

I had applied for life insurance. Felt like the responsible thing to do. Adult stuff. Boring. Necessary. I thought I'd sign some forms, let them draw a little blood, pay the premium, and forget about it.

"We regret to inform you…"

I read that line three times. Slow. Behind it was a lab sheet and a note: "Follow up with your physician." I didn't have a physician. I had a barber. A mechanic. A keyboard dealer I trusted more than most people. A "physician" sounded like someone you see when things are already broken.

But there it was. Things were broken.

When I saw the numbers, I didn't even fully understand them. A memory hit me from 1979. I was about to graduate from high school. Had won a college scholarship. Needed a physical. The doctor, with kind eyes and a quiet voice, looked at my results and said, "You're borderline diabetic."

I was young. Moving fast. Full of plans. "Borderline" didn't scare me. Felt like being near a highway but not on it. I nodded. Said I'd "watch it." Then watched nothing.

Now, that moment came back without the kindness.

I made the appointment.

The doctor's office was bright in that way that makes you squint. The paper on the table cracked under me when I moved. A poster of the digestive system hung crooked. A plastic heart sat on the counter like a paperweight with tubes. I felt like a kid waiting for a shot, and I've always hated needles.

The doctor walked in with my chart, and that calm some doctors carry the kind that makes you nervous and grateful. She introduced herself. Asked how I'd been feeling.

"Fine," I said. Too fast.

She raised an eyebrow like she'd heard that before.

"We ran your panels," she said, sitting. "Your fasting glucose is elevated. Your A1C shows Type 2 diabetes."

She didn't say maybe. Didn't say borderline. She said it.

I tried to nod like this was about car tires or taxes. "Okay," I said. "What does that mean... day to day?"

"It means," she said gently, "your blood sugar has been high for a while. But it also means we can do a lot starting now to bring it down. Diet changes. Movement. Maybe medication. We'll get you a meter so you can check at home."

My mind flashed to my dad pricking his finger every day. One drop of blood on a strip. To know.

There's a certain weight that settles in a room when something changes. I felt it then. Under her words was a simple truth: nothing in my life would be casual anymore.

She must have seen something cross my face. Her voice softened. "This isn't punishment. It's information. And information is power."

I thought, Information can also feel like guilt.

She kept going. Calm. "We'll start you on a low dose of medication. You'll meet with our diabetes educator. He'll show you how to use the meter. What the numbers mean. We'll repeat labs in three months."

Three months. Felt like forever. Also, not enough time.

"Any questions?" she asked.

I had a thousand. Only one came out. "Is this… my fault?"

She took a breath. Tilted her head. "It's not that simple. Genetics. Lifestyle. Environment. All play a part. Your dad had diabetes, yes?"

I nodded.

"That matters. But what matters now," she said, tapping the chart, "is that we start writing a new chapter. You're not behind. You're starting."

I wanted to believe her. I also wanted to hand the chart back and go back to the old story.

In the pharmacy aisle, everything sounded like static. Meters in blue boxes promised accuracy. Lancets lined up like tiny weapons. Strips in little bottles said they'd "fit most meters." None of them said what I wanted: You can go back.

A tech showed me how to load the lancet. "Adjust the depth here," she said. Click. "You don't need to hurt yourself to get a drop." She smiled. Like it was funny. I didn't laugh.

Back in the car, I sat with the meter in my lap. Screen blank. Waiting. Felt like a judge. I pricked my finger. The sting surprised me sharply. Quick. Real. A red bead formed. I touched it to the strip. Watched the countdown: 5… 4… 3… 2… 1.

The number appeared. Higher than I hoped. Lower than I feared. But still, it felt like a verdict.

I thought about that kid again. The one getting ready for college. The "borderline" boy who nodded at the doctor said he'd watch it, then walked away and forgot. I have been thinking about all the prayers for safety since then. For the purpose. For music to mean something. I thought about the crashes in the hospital rooms. Nurses are feeding me ice cream to make me laugh. Felicia was writing my parents' number on her arm with my blood. I thought about God, whether he was listening now, in this car with a meter in my lap, the screen blank, waiting like an unblinking eye.

"Help," I whispered. Not fancy. Just true.

The diabetes educator's office felt warmer than the clinic. He had a whiteboard. A smile that didn't feel forced. "I'm Dennis," he said, drawing a circle and dividing it into pieces. "This is your plate. We're going to talk about carbs."

To me, carbs meant bread. Turns out, carbs meant almost everything. He held up a plastic apple. Then a tiny scoop of rice. "Both count," he said. "Just differently."

He wrote on the board: 15 grams equals one serving. Letters neat. "I don't want you starving," he said. "I want you to plan. Food isn't the enemy. Mindlessness is."

I took notes like I was back in school. He walked me through breakfast choices, when to check, and what to do if the number was high. "Don't panic," he said. "Data, not drama."

Before I left, he looked at me, not the chart, not the meter, me. "You look like a man who takes care of others," he said. "Make room to take care of yourself."

That hit me. Brought back something my little brother always told me: "Like those folks say on the plane, put on your oxygen mask first, then help others." He'd challenge me: How can you help anyone if you don't take care of your own health first? And he was right. Always.

Something in me softened. I hadn't even realized how tight I'd been holding my breath.

At home, a new routine took shape. The meter case unzipped with a quiet sigh. The lancet clicked into place. A test strip out of its small, expensive vial. Morning, Before meals, Two hours after, Night. My days began shaping themselves around numbers and alarms.

I learned the words: fasting, postprandial, A1C, and target range. Learned the sounds: the beep when it worked, the soft curse when it didn't. The quiet "thank you" when the number wasn't bad.

I changed what I could. Fewer late-night snacks. More water. Walks that started as punishment turned into moving prayer. I learned to listen to my body like a musician learns a room. Too high felt buzzy. Scattered. Too low felt like the floor dropped out.

I told myself I'd keep the lows down with planning the highs with discipline. Then life reminded me it doesn't follow rules.

One afternoon, between rehearsal and a concert, I checked. Saw a number that made my stomach drop. I'd eaten right. Walked. Done everything "correct." But there it was high. Unmoved by my effort.

First feeling: shame. Second: anger. Third: I breathed.

"Data, not drama," I heard Dennis say. I drank water. Took a walk. The number came down. Not a win. Just a step.

At my three-month follow-up, the doctor read the screen. "Your A1C today is 7.5, down from 8.1." He looked up. Smiled. "Headed in the right direction. Good work."

I wanted confetti. Instead, I nodded. Asked what "good work" meant tomorrow.

He reviewed my meds. Checked my feet. Listened to my heart. "I'd like to keep an eye on your blood pressure," he said, almost casually. Ordered more lab tests I didn't know about: microalbumin and creatinine. I wrote them down. Didn't know then how much those words would matter later.

When I stood to leave, he put a hand on the back of the chair. "How are you doing?"
Not your numbers. You.

The question went deep. "Some days I feel like me," I said. "Some days I feel like… a chart."

He nodded. Like he'd heard it before and still cared. "You are not your numbers," he said. "Even when they're loud."

It took me a while to tell my mom. Not because I didn't trust her. Because I did, I knew how it would land. She had sung faith into our mornings, prayed for us through every scare. Believed someone would play her piano long before I existed. I didn't want to see her flinch at the word diabetes.

When I finally called my mom, she didn't gasp. Didn't preach. She hummed low, like she was finding her note, then said, "JayDee, we'll walk this together." Pots clinked in the background, the familiar sound of her kitchen. "You eat, you move, you pray. You hear me?"

"I hear you," I said. And I did. Her voice pulled something back into place inside me that had started to come apart.

Later that night, I sat at the piano. Let my hands find their way. The melody that came wasn't strong. Wasn't triumphant. It was stubborn. Held one note too long, then moved when it was ready. I stayed with it until the room changed. Until the sound made space big enough for both fear and faith to stand side by side without pushing each other out.

That melody became something more. A music composition I later named "When God Hears." In that moment, I was asking God to hear me as I prayed. Not just with words. Many people say you have to speak out loud for God to listen to you. That never felt right to me. I've always known He hears whether I'm speaking, playing, or just sitting quietly with my heart open.

But there was a difference. I didn't always feel Him hearing. But when He did it, it was powerful. Real. When God Hears became an anthem for the prayers that come through keys, through silence, through tears.

Then came another appointment with an ophthalmologist. No soft talk. He looked into my dilated eye, turned off the light, and said, "There's damage. We need to watch this closely."

My mind went back to the last car crash. The doctors then told me about the orbital fracture. Said there was a forty percent chance I'd lose vision in my left eye. Now, he told me I had Proliferative Diabetic Retinopathy PDR. Bleeding in the back of the eye, moving fast. That explained the floaters. The flashes. The streaks. I was going blind. On top of that, mild cataracts.

I drove home with the world blurred from the drops. Fought tears, knew they'd make it worse. I didn't tell my mom. Didn't tell my wife. Didn't tell anyone for days. I prayed. Then cried. Then prayed again.

My thoughts ran in circles: Why let me survive two wrecks, only to be undone by my own blood? Why are my eyes the ones I needed to teach, to play, to write music?

I wish I could say I got an answer. I didn't. What I got was a different kind of prayer. Not "Fix it." But "Be with me in it." Not "Take it away." But "Help me live with what this means."

When I finally said it out loud, it didn't feel like giving up. It felt like the first honest thing I'd said in a long time.

I started laser therapy to destroy abnormal blood vessels and stop more bleeding. That's what was causing the floaters and flashes. He also began a series of PAVBLU injections to shrink those vessels and prevent them from leaking.

I started talking to God the way I used to speak to the cross on the hill as a boy. Simple. Messy. Not rehearsed. I told Him when I was scared, when I was grateful, when I was angry, when I was nervous.

Faith, I realized, wasn't that shiny picture from Sunday school. It was a thread I kept pulling through each day, so everything didn't fall apart.

Church still mattered. Songs still felt like home. But my faith became less about the building. More about breathing. Less about looking strong. More about being honest enough to heal.

I began to understand what my father had shown me when I returned to St. Mark A.M.E. after many years away. Faith isn't performance. Its presence.

One quiet afternoon, I opened a box of old photos. One fell out of me at ten, skinny, grinning in front of a piano too big for my size. My brother and I outside our home near the corner, the sun stretching shadows across the block. We didn't know how fast life could change.

I sat with that box for a long time. Something in me softened.

After the crashes, I said, "God must have loved me," as if I were daring anyone to argue. Now, those words didn't feel like defiance. They felt like a choice. Made every day. Not because the road was easy. But because I kept walking it.

The meter will beep again in a few hours. The strip will take another drop. The number will be what it is.

And I'll do what I can, one honest step at a time: eat, move, pray, play, rest. Repeat.

Information, not indictment. Data, not drama. Presence, not performance.

A new chapter. Even if I write it one small paragraph at a time.

Reflection

The diagnosis didn't come with trumpets. No lightning. Just quiet words on official paper. Numbers glowing on a small screen. The sting of a lancet is now part of my daily routine.

At first, diabetes felt like a verdict. Final. Heavy.

But slowly, through the doctor's advice, my brother's reminders, my mother's voice, and the music that still came out of me, not despite this, but because of it, I began to see it differently.

Faith wasn't about pretending the numbers didn't matter. It was about refusing to let them define me.

Each time I pricked my finger, it became less like punishment and more like prayer. A way of saying: I'm still here. Still aware. Still choosing to live.

The boy who ignored "borderline" had become the man learning to walk within the borders of discipline, of faith, of grace.

CHAPTER 12

The Cumulative Toll of Illness

All the affirmations. All the mantras I repeated to myself. None of it prepared me for what came next.

I had had diabetes for years, unchecked and unmanaged. Now, the signs of kidney damage were showing up. My primary care doctor reviewed a fresh set of labs and gave me that look that doctors get when the news isn't good. I felt the room start to fade. Like, I was going black right there.

When I first heard "renal failure," the room tilted. I was on an exam table. The physician's assistant looked me in the eye.

"You're going to need to see a specialist. Soon."

I watched her lips move. The words hung in the air like they were in another language, just like when I stepped off the plane in Japan, surrounded by sounds I couldn't understand. But this wasn't excitement. This was fear under fluorescent lights.

"Specialist for what?" I asked. My voice cracked more than I wanted.

"For your kidneys," she said gently. "Your labs show they're failing. You need to get ahead of this now. A nephrologist is the best step."

I told her I would. Didn't even know what a nephrologist was. Didn't fully grasp how serious this was.

Then she saw my face. My body language. Knew I didn't get it.

She leaned in. "You really need to see a kidney specialist." My eyes widened. She could tell I was scared.

And I was. Because I remembered what my doctor had told me before about how diabetes can damage the kidneys. I knew it was dangerous.

The nurse practitioner must have sensed how much I didn't want to believe it. So she added, "It may be nothing. But it's better to check."

I told her I would. She said I should go sooner rather than later. I promised I'd make the appointment that week.

I didn't.

I had a concert scheduled in Oklahoma City. I told myself I'd go, play, enjoy the trip, then come home and make the call.

But the whole time, my mind wasn't steady. One minute, I'd feel okay. The following thoughts swarmed too many to catch. Too heavy to ignore.

The Shadow of Diabetes

I thought back to the doctor in 1979. I was just out of high school. She looked at my labs and said, "You're borderline diabetic." At the time, I didn't take it seriously. I was young. Seemed healthy. Chasing scholarships. Music gigs. Focused on what was next.

Diabetes? That was for older people. Not me.

Now, here I was, mid-thirties, hearing words like renal failure and dialysis. My body was paying for choices I made years ago. Bad habits. Ignoring warnings. Thinking I was bulletproof.

Faith without action. Health without care.

My body wasn't asking anymore. It was telling.

Going to Oklahoma and Back

In late October 2014, I boarded a Southwest Airbus to Oklahoma City. I hadn't flown in a while and had to face that fear all over again, being up in the air, trusting metal and weather and pilots. But this time, the fear of flying wasn't as intense as it usually was.

Because something heavier was on my mind.

I had a plan. A mental schedule. A reason. My mission? To go to Oklahoma City, do the show, enjoy myself while I could, so when I got back home, I'd be ready to start dialysis if I had to.

That thought of dialysis filled my head so much that there was no room left for fear of the plane.

Funny how the mind works. Even against itself.

I remember stepping off the plane. Oklahoma heat hit me fast. I wondered: Do I look sick? Can people tell? The other musicians didn't know. They laughed, joked, and carried their gear as if it were just another gig. I watched them, then pulled myself back to why I was there.

In my hotel room, I started rehearsing. Didn't think I'd be able to focus. But I did. Better than I expected.

On stage, I smiled. Played strongly. Carried my part. Off stage, I carried something else in silence.

The Langston University Homecoming event was alive. The food was good. The crowd buzzed. There was a real sense of community, people singing, hugging, catching up like they'd known each other forever.

I even met Charles Barkley. That was surreal. At six-foot-three, I always pictured him towering. But in person, he wasn't that much taller than me,a down-to-earth guy. We had fun during sound check, maybe more than during the actual show. People kept sneaking in to hear us warm up. Felt like we were already performing.

That night, the energy was even higher. I met Rodney Peete and Holly Robinson Peete. Both were kind. Both smiled easily. Onstage, everything came together. For a few hours, I wasn't thinking about doctors. Wasn't thinking about labs or kidneys. I was playing.

But in the quiet moment's backstage, in the hotel room, on the shuttle ride, the nurse practitioner's words would come back: You really need to see a specialist. It may be nothing… but you should check it out.

The quieter I got, the louder those words became.

The flight home felt heavier than the one there. I couldn't push it away anymore. I knew it was on me now to make the call. To get the appointment. To face what might be true.

I didn't want to know. But I also knew that not knowing could cost me.

Oklahoma gave me music. Good moments. Memories I still carry. But it also sent me home with a decision I could no longer avoid.

And one truth stayed with me: I hadn't started dialysis yet. But the warning had already begun.

The Clinic

When I got home from Oklahoma, my suitcase didn't even make it past the front door before reality caught up. The nurse practitioner's words weren't in the background anymore. They were right there, loud and clear.

I told myself I'd call the specialist tomorrow. But tomorrow never came. One day passed. Then two. Then a week.

Finally, I picked up the phone: the nephrologist's office scheduled labs and a consultation. I went in thinking this would be routine, maybe a diet change, a new pill, then I'd go on with life.

Instead, it was the day everything changed.

The results were precise: my kidneys weren't just struggling. They were failing. Not at risk. Not something to watch. Failing.

The doctor said my kidney function had dropped so low that dialysis had to start now.

I sat there. Nodded like I understood. But the words didn't feel real. Dialysis was for other people. Older people. People who looked sick. Not me. Not someone still teaching music, still playing gigs, still writing songs, still trying to live his life.

But the truth wasn't in how I felt. It was in the chart. Numbers in black and white that didn't care about my plans.

Choosing a Modality

The nephrologist slid a packet across the desk. "You'll need to choose a modality," he said.

Just the word 'modality' sounded foreign, like something I wasn't meant to understand. He explained the options: hemodialysis at a center, three times a week. Or peritoneal dialysis at home every night.

I went home that day and looked up pictures online. People on dialysis. Hooked to machines. The faces stared back at me. Hollow cheeks. Tired eyes. Tubes running from their arms. Zombies, my mind whispered. I hated myself for thinking it.

But the fear was stronger than guilt.

The Surgeries

I chose peritoneal dialysis. They said it would give me freedom. I could do it at home, overnight, no clinic chair. No long days hooked up during the week.

But freedom came with a cost.

I went through three surgeries to get the catheter placed right in my abdomen. Each one meant weeks of healing. Learning how to move without pulling on the wound. Bandages taped across my stomach. Tenderness, I had to live with every second.

Then came the training classes. Sterilizing everything, mixing solutions, and practicing connections on a dummy machine. Linda and Deeana, my dialysis nurses, were clear: "One slip-up, and you could get an infection. And that could mean hospitalization or worse."

They didn't yell it. Just said it calmly. That made it hit harder.

Linda was the nurse my nephrologist assigned to me. She softened the edges. Explained things in a way I could understand. Made me feel like I wasn't broken, just learning.

At first, the process was slow. Awkward. Something is humbling about hooking yourself to a machine that keeps you alive.

The first night at home, I sat on the edge of my bed, staring at the setup. Clear plastic bags of fluid. Sterile caps. The machine hums quietly, but is present. This thing would be with me every night for years.

In the clinic, the smell hit first, bleach. Antiseptic. Something sharp that stayed in your clothes. Then the sound of the hum of machines. Not like amps warming up before a set. This was cold. Mechanical. Pumps moving blood in and out of bodies too tired to fight.

The people got to me the most. Some are in wheelchairs. Others shuffling slowly. Eyes empty. Like they were halfway gone. Still breathing, but not really here.

Every time I walked into that clinic, I froze at the door. Man, God... I don't belong here.

Linda always saw it. She'd walk over, voice kind but steady, like she'd done this a hundred times. "You'll get used to it. Everyone feels nervous at first."

I wanted to tell her she was wrong. I'd never get used to it. But all I did was nod.

Callback: Remembering Age Thirteen

That smell of antiseptic. The sight of the machines. The slow shuffle of feet. It pulled me back to when I was thirteen, lying in a hospital bed after the car hit me.

Back then, the hospital felt different. I was hurt. Concussed. Stitches in my head. But there was still something innocent in me. Nurses joked with me. A janitor raced me down the hall in my wheelchair, pretending his mop was a horse. The man in the next bed turned out to be Dan Rowan; he made me laugh even when I didn't feel like it.

Even in pain, there was light.

But here? Now? Standing in a dialysis clinic? No laughter. No races down the hall. No jokes from the next bed.

Just the hum of machines. Bodies are worn down. Eyes that had seen too much. And the quiet knowing: this isn't temporary. This is how life is now.

The thirteen-year-old walked out of that hospital believing he'd get strong again. Thinking time would fix things. The man I was now stood in the doorway, realizing some things don't come back.

And that truth, so quiet, so final, hit me like a sucker punch all over again.

The Surgeon's Warning

There was one surgeon, years after my second car wreck, who sat me down in his office. His words came back now, clear as if he were still in the room:

"There's about a 40% chance you could lose sight in your left eye."

I had cried for days after that and prayed until my throat hurt. Bargained with God like it was a deal we could negotiate. Felt like He'd already asked too much. I didn't tell my parents. I was too afraid.

Now, sitting in the dialysis clinic for my bi-monthly appointments, the same cracks in my faith started opening again. Why would this happen? Haven't I been through enough? Haven't I tried to do right?

I thought about all the times I stayed away from trouble. I made the choices I did because I wanted to be "good." I used to believe faith was like a balance sheet, good deeds on one side, failures on the other. That if I did enough right, life would stay fair.

But here I was. Facing a machine. Facing a future I didn't choose. Learning that faith doesn't work like math.

Ten Hours a Night

Treatment meant long nights every night. No breaks. The machine sat in the corner of my room, blinking lights like it was alive. I'd hook up, watch the fluid go in, feel the pressure build in my stomach, then wait as it drained out. Six. Seven cycles. Ten hours. Night after night.

Some nights, the pain in my abdomen was too much. Other nights, I lie there, staring at the ceiling. Couldn't sleep.

I felt tied down like I was floating, but couldn't move like an astronaut on a short cord.

My wife's friends bought me a big recliner chair as a gift. Thought it would help me rest better. It did some. Not much. Comfort had become something I remembered, not something I felt.

What kept me sane was music. Not the loud kind. Not stage lights or applause. None of that. Late at night, I played quiet, thoughtful music. Soft piano. Slow strings. The kind that calms your breath. Reminds you there's still beauty even when your body feels like it's turning against you.

Good Morning, Mr. Bruce

One night, I couldn't sleep. My mind went to Mr. Sidney J. Bruce, my first piano teacher. He didn't just teach me notes. He taught me discipline. How to respect the music. How to respect myself.

In his honor, I wrote a piece titled "Good Morning, Mr. Bruce." Every note felt like I was talking to him. Like I was saying, thank you for showing me music wasn't just sound. It could save you.

Even with tubes in my stomach. Even with pain in my side. That song gave me back a little of my dignity.

Remember When We Remembered

Another piece came later: Remember When We Remembered. It grew out of grief. Out of missing my father. Out of the ache from losing parts of myself to illness. Writing felt like opening a window in a room with no air.

Each note carried memory. Each chord carried faith, not polished. Not perfect. But scarred. Limping. The kind of faith that still gets up even after being sucker punched.

Faith on Life Support

Dialysis didn't just drain my body. It drained my faith.
I used to think faith was a shield, something that would stop the pain before it hit.

Now I learned it wasn't a shield at all. It was a lifeline. Thin. Stretching, but still holding even when I was gasping for air.

Some nights, I thought faith was gone. Other nights, it was the only thing keeping me from pulling the tubes out and walking away.

But in the middle of that slow, hard season, faith changed for me. It wasn't about one prayer and then a miracle falling from the sky. It was about praying silently a thousand times, and still choosing to hook up the machine the next night.

It wasn't flashy. It wasn't loud. It was survival. It was resistance. It was faith.

Reflection

The toll of illness isn't just broken bones or tired organs. It's broken illusions. Broken pride. The loss of what you thought was certain.

But if I've learned anything, it's this: broken doesn't mean useless.

It means rebuilt.

When I was thirteen, lying in that hospital bed, head stitched, body sore, it wasn't the medicine that reminded me I was alive. It was the nurses laughing with me. The janitor is racing my wheelchair down the hall. The man in the next bed turned out to be a comedian who made me smile when I didn't want to.

Those small things. Almost silly. But they broke through the fear.

Decades later, hooked to a dialysis machine, it was music that did the same. Writing Good Morning, Mr. Bruce. Remember When We Remembered. Those songs gave me something to hold onto when everything else felt gone.

The notes became that janitor's mop stick, pretending he was on a horse. The melodies became the nurse slipping me extra ice cream. The silence between chords became proof I was still breathing.

That's what faith looked like then. Not big miracles. Not instant healing. But small mercies dressed as music. As memory. As breath.

Night after night, tied to that machine, I kept writing. Kept creating. Kept breathing.

And somewhere between pain and prayer, in the quiet hum of the pump, I realized:

This part of it would become part of the story,the story of getting sucker punched, again and again, and still choosing to stand back up.

CHAPTER 13

Dialysis Nights

The machine hummed like it was alive. Eventually, I moved it into the corner of my studio. Pale blue light glows in the dark. At two in the morning, it was the only thing awake. Its screen casts shadows across cables, sheet music, and the worn carpet.

This wasn't how I thought my nights would be, not hooked to tubes. Not counting time in liters and cycles, and not hearing alarms instead of applause.

When I first started peritoneal dialysis, putting it in the bedroom seemed practical. But I didn't stay blind to what it was doing to my wife. Every time the alarm went off sharp, loud, like something that wouldn't stop, she'd wake up. Roll over. Half-asleep but alert.

I hated seeing her carry my sickness, even in her sleep.

So one night, I unplugged everything and moved it all into my studio. The same room where I wrote music. Where I studied, prayed. Tried to disappear into sound.

Now it has become my clinic. My sanctuary turned sickroom. My stage turned ward.

Even the oversized recliner they gave me was brought in there. I told myself I'd rest better here. Wanted to believe it. Some nights, I did. Other nights, the tubes still pulled at my side no matter how I sat. The catheter reminded me deep in the skin that my body wasn't entirely mine anymore.

The Noise of Survival

The machine had its own language. I had to learn it.
A soft hiss meant fluid was moving. A long whine meant the cycle had paused. A sudden, sharp, high-pitched alarm meant something was wrong. Or just thought it was.

Sometimes the solution drained too fast. Pulled at my stomach. Cramps shot into my legs. Other times, the flow slowed. The pump strained. The alarm went off. I'd wake up half-asleep, fumble with the tubing, praying I wouldn't have to restart the whole thing. My studio was filled with those sounds until silence felt strange.

The tubing ran long across the floor, past the piano keyboards, all the way to the bathroom. More than once, I turned too fast, and it tangled. I'd curse low, untangle it, then remind myself: Don't move too much.

I learned to sit still. Not because I was calm. Because I had to.

Then there was the dryness. Dialysis didn't just take out toxins. It took moisture. My skin cracked on my arms. My legs flaked white, no matter how much lotion I used. Bottles sat everywhere by the recliner, by the machine, even next to the piano and keyboards.

Some nights, after hooking up, I'd rub lotion on my calves while the machine hummed. A small thing. But it felt like one choice I still had to make.

The Body Keeps Score

No one tells you how much dialysis changes your body. It doesn't just treat you. It rewires you.

The catheter stayed in my side like something that didn't belong. Tender. Sore. Even after months, it still felt foreign.

Sleep became trial and error. Try lying on the left too much pressure. The right-side tube pinches. On my back line pulls. In the end, the recliner was the only thing that worked, and even that failed me most nights. Cramps would hit at three in the morning, sharp and sudden.

Sometimes the fluid came in so fast it felt like someone was twisting my stomach out like a wet towel. Other nights, the pain moved down my legs, locking them up. I'd rub them hard, whispering, "Come on, come on," like I could talk my muscles into working again.

I tried to laugh at myself. I, sitting there in the middle of the night, rubbing lotion on my arms like it was some ritual. But the laugh never lasted. It dropped fast.

Truth is, I hated it. Hated the tubes. Hated the alarms. Hated how my life was now counted in cycles, in liters, in beeps.

Alone Together

Even in my studio, I wasn't alone. My wife would check on me. Quiet. Slow. Not wanting to wake me if I'd finally fallen asleep. Sometimes she'd stand in the doorway, just a shadow against the light from the hall. She never said much. Never complained. But I could see in her stillness what it cost her to see me like that.

I carried guilt as heavy as the machine. She didn't sign up for this. Nobody did. And still, there she was. Steady. Her silence wasn't empty. It was a faith, quiet and deep, holding me up when mine broke.

But most nights, it was just me. Sitting in that recliner at 3 a.m., hooked up, still. Alone with the man inside the one full of doubt. Anger. Questions.

"God, is this really it? Is this what faith gets me? Tubes in my stomach and alarms all night?"

Some nights, I prayed loudly. Angry. Wanting answers. Other nights, I didn't pray at all. Too tired. Too empty. Couldn't even form the words.

And the silence always answered back. Not with peace. With weight. Heavier than the cramps. Heavier than the tubing. Heavier than I thought I could carry.

Faith Tested in the Quiet Hours

There was one night I'll never forget. The alarm went off loudly, screaming. I stumbled to fix it. My side cramped so hard I thought I'd pass out. I sat there, bent over, sweat running down my face, whispering, "I can't do this anymore."

And in that moment, I remembered the doctor's words from years before: "You don't want to end up in a dialysis chair. Get your stuff together." Her voice came back clear, like something I should've listened to. Back then, I brushed it off. Thought I was too strong. Too young. Too busy living to slow down.

Now, here I was hooked to a machine in my own studio, and her warning settled deep in my chest.

The machine beeped again. Insistent. Needing me. I wiped my face, tired, hurting, and let out a curse, then a prayer, all in the same breath.

Music in the Wreckage

If anything saved me during those nights, it was music. I'd play it for hours: jazz, ambient, gospel, new age, lo-fi. Anything that could break the silence. Anything that felt alive.

Some nights, I wrote music while the machine hummed beside me like an unwanted metronome keeping time. Other nights, I just listened. Let the sound fill the room. Let it move through me, as if it were feeding my blood.

Music was the only thing that made me feel human when the machine made me feel like a patient. Like a case. Like something being fixed.

It reminded me I was still more than my body. Still more than tubes. Still more than cycles.

The Grind

Ten hours. Every night. No breaks. That was the deal.

The machine didn't care if I was tired. Suppose I had work in the morning if my spirit was worn down to nothing. It just needed me to connect.

There were nights I thought about unhooking. I said this earlier. Just pulling the tubes out and walking away. Pretending I was free.

But pretending wasn't freedom. It was a surrender. And I wasn't ready to give up.

So I kept going. Night after night. Plugged in. Showing up.

It wasn't glamorous. Wasn't holy. Wasn't brave or noble. It was just survival.

And maybe just maybe that was enough.

Reflection

Dialysis stripped me down to the raw edges of being human.

It wasn't the kind of trial people clap for. Not the type that gets shared from a pulpit. It was the kind that leaves you awake at three in the morning, whispering prayers under the hum of a machine. Bargaining. Begging. Sometimes just breathing.

Some nights, surviving felt like losing. Other nights, it was the only win I had.

What I learned in those hours is this: faith isn't proven in front of crowds. It's tested in silence. In cramps. In alarms that only you can hear.

And even hooked to tubes and pain, even when my body felt broken, Faith still found a way to answer not with thunder, but with a whisper: Not finished. Still standing.

CHAPTER 14

Faith Rebuilt, Faith Renewed

By the time I reached this part of my life, faith wasn't something I heard in sermons or songs. It wasn't floating anymore. It was bruised. Bent. Tested in the quietest, most brutal ways. Dialysis nights. Dreams I had to let go. A body that didn't feel like mine.

But still, there was a small fire inside. Stubborn. Not bright. But glowing.

I stopped asking God to fix everything. Instead, I asked Him to change me. To make me stronger. Wiser. Strong enough to face what wouldn't ever change.

Michael Jackson's voice would come back to me: "I'm starting with the man in the mirror… I'm asking him to change his ways." That song became mine. My family knew it. My friends, too. Every time it played, someone would look at me, smile, and say, "There's your song."

They weren't wrong.

When those words came on, it felt like holding up a mirror. I couldn't stop dialysis.

Couldn't take the tubes out and be free. But I could decide how I carried it.

And that made all the difference.

My Grandmother's Voice

It was during this season that my maternal grandmother carried me through.

She was the one who called me "Preacher." As a boy with a speech impediment, I'd repeat myself, trying to get the words right. My little brother would step in and translate for me when others didn't understand. But Grandmom never laughed. Never rushed me. She'd smile and say, "Preacher, keep on talking. You'll get it right."

Her house had smells I still carry: collard greens simmering, Turnip greens with that peppery bite. Mustard greens cooked slowly and deeply. Rich. Savory. No need for sugar or bribes. I cleaned my plate every time.

She loved her garden. I can still see her bent in the backyard, apron tied tight, hands dark with dirt, pulling weeds with one hand, tamping soil down with the other. Rows of greens swaying in the breeze, her pride. Her work.

When I came to her hurt or discouraged, she'd look me in the eye and say, "Preacher, things are going to work out. They always do."

Not loud. Not flashy. Just steady.

Her prayers were like that, too quiet, soft, but powerful. Real. You could feel them.

Her favorite song was "There Is a Name." Whenever they asked her to sing in church, that's what she'd give.

I sang at her funeral. Didn't know it then, but that day was practice for this season of my life. Standing in front of people. Voice shaking. Hurting, but still singing.

That's what dialysis felt like: trembling, broken, but refusing to be silent.

The sanctuary smelled both sweet and heavy that day. Pews creaked under the weight of mourners. My cousin had just finished singing. Pastors sat in their robes. Then I stood. Began "There Is a Name." My voice broke. For a second, I wanted to stop. To walk away.

Then I saw my mother. She nodded. Just once. But it was enough.

This was the same song I heard her sing at that small church on 53rd Street when I was a boy. I closed my eyes. Sang through the tears.

That day, I learned something: faith isn't about hitting every note right. It's about not stopping in the middle of the song.

People wept. And I felt her there like she was standing beside me, whispering again: "Preacher, things are going to work out. They always do."

I still say those words today. Not because life is easy. But because she taught me to believe them. Things are going to work out. Because they always do.

One of my clearest memories goes back to when I was six. I asked her how the world got dark at night. She smiled, pulled me close, and said, "God has a big blanket. When it's time for His children to rest, He lays it over the earth so they can sleep."

For years, I believed that blanket was real. Not pretend. Not a story. I pictured it soft, wide, covering everything. Even after I grew old enough to understand it was her way of tucking me in, I kept that image. God was pulling darkness over the world like a cover, so that I could rest.

That blanket came back to me many nights, hooked to the dialysis machine, staring at the blue glow of the monitor at 2 a.m.

In those quiet hours, I'd feel it again, not on my skin, but in my spirit, like God hadn't forgotten me, like he was still covering me. Even now.

Faith Rebuilt

So, little by little, piece by piece, faith started coming back.

Not in big miracles. Not in sudden healing or walking away from dialysis, free. But in the quiet grit of getting through the night. In the memory of my grandmother's soft prayers. In the smell of mustard greens cooking slowly in her kitchen. In that old image of God pulling His blanket across the sky so His children could sleep.

It came in the blue glow of the machine at 2 a.m. In the hum of tubing. In Michael Jackson's voice, reminding me: start with the man in the mirror.

Faith stopped being just something I believed. It became something I lived. Something I carried. Like a muscle built over time. Like scar tissue after a wound.

It wasn't perfect. It wasn't clean. But it was mine.

And as I sat in my studio night after night, listening to the hiss and hum of the machine, I realized something my grandmother had been right all along: Things are going to work out. Because they always do.

Not because life is easy. But because faith, even when broken, can still grow back stronger.

Reflection

Faith isn't rebuilt in one big moment. It comes back in pieces.

A whisper from my grandmother: "Things are going to work out." The smell of greens cooking slowly on the stove. That old picture in my mind of God laying His blanket over the sky so His children can sleep.

It comes in the form of a song, "Man in the Mirror," calling me to change what I can when everything else is out of my hands.

For me, it came back in the hum of the dialysis machine at 2 a.m. In choosing not to quit. Not to stop halfway through the song.

That's when I learned: renewal doesn't mean no scars. It means carrying them without shame and still saying, deep in your chest: Things are going to work out. Because they always do.

CHAPTER 15

Still Standing

I'm sitting in my home studio, headphones on, working on a new cue for a library producer. Needs to be fast. Action-packed. The monitors glow softly in the dim room. The sequencer moves forward with every note I add.

It feels surreal. For years, I didn't think I'd ever be here again, making music like this. With focus. With purpose. Dialysis nights made me doubt it. Hospital stays made me question if I'd ever have the strength. Even after the transplant, as grateful as I am, I wasn't sure what kind of man I'd be left standing.

But here I am. Still creating. Still here.

It's been over five years since the transplant. No infections. No rejection scares, no close calls with losing the gift that saved me. The only real test since then was COVID-19.

Not a surprise punch. One I saw coming, watching it move across the world like a storm. When it hit me, it knocked me down. But this time, I wasn't caught off guard.

I'd lived through enough to know how to get back up.

The Body's Scars, the Spirit's Strength

Diabetes and dialysis took more from me than I can ever put into words. I carry what they left behind in my body, in my bones. Not just the scars, but the tiredness that never entirely goes away. The ache that shows up on cold mornings. The quiet reminders that this body has been through war after war.

But scars aren't the same as defeat.

I don't dwell on those nights. I choose not to go back there. Instead, I fill my mind with what's ahead in days at the beach. Quiet dinners with my wife. Time with the grandkids. A future where laughter is louder than lab results.

I'm not all the way there yet. But I can see the road now. It's not flat. It's not easy.
But it's going up. And for the first time in a long time, it feels like a promise, not a threat.

Faith in Real Time

My faith today isn't the same as it was when I was young. It's not clean. Not polished. Not perfect. It's not about pretending I don't doubt. Or that I'm never tired. It's about standing faith, the kind that shows up worn, bruised, but still here. Still willing to rise.

I used to think faith was a shield. Something that would block the blows. I know better now. It doesn't keep the sucker punches from landing. It's what you hold onto when they do, when the air gets knocked out of you. When you're flat on the mat, not sure you've got another try in you.

That's where I am today. Not invincible. But resilient. Not untouched. But unbroken.

Music as Evidence

If you want to know how I made it through, listen to my music.

My wife says it's like my girlfriend. Not in a jealous way. She says it with respect. Because she knows it's been there every step of the way. When I was on dialysis, when I couldn't sleep, when I didn't have words, music never left.

When I sit at the piano or work in my studio, I'm not just playing. I'm dreaming.

Every note holds a piece of the story of the hospital nights. The tears I wiped away before anyone saw. The laughter that surprised me when I thought I had none left. The quiet prayers I whispered into the dark.

Music doesn't just prove I survived; it proves I'm alive. It proves survival can still be beautiful.

Family & Legacy

These days, when my grandchildren come over, I watch them the way I used to look at that cross on the hill as a boy. Full of wonder. They don't know everything I've been through. Don't need to. What matters is that they see me here. Still present. Still loving them. Still walking.

I think about my dad's words: "Take care of your mom." I think of my mom, still singing, her voice just as steady as it's always been. I think of my grandmothers, one pointing me toward the cross, the other smiling softly and saying, "Preacher, things are going to work out. They always do."

They were all right. Things did work out. Not how I planned. Not without pain. Not without scars. But in a way that showed me faith doesn't end with one person. It carries forward.

Now, waiting for my second grandson to be born, I feel the shift again, not just in time, but in purpose. Birth. Life. Legacy. All woven together into something more profound than I ever understood as that boy by the cross, or that man hooked to a machine under hospital lights.

Faith isn't just surviving. It's passing on.

Reflection

I've been sucker punched in my faith over and over. Again. And again. And still, this is where I stand: Not perfect. Not unscarred. But alive. Faithful. Still standing.

If I can make it through, so can you. Please believe that. Not because I'm strong. Because I kept going, one breath, one night, one prayer at a time.

CHAPTER 16

Legacy & Lessons

If there's one thing I want my children and grandchildren to know, it's this: I love you. Deeply. Fiercely. Imperfectly.

I wish I'd made better choices when I was younger, ones that looked further ahead, toward the lives you'd live. Too often, I poured myself into building other people's dreams, while mine waited. I didn't lay enough bricks for the future that would be yours.

But even in that, I want you to know this: You come from strong people.

I've traced our family back to the early 1800s. Men and women you'll never meet but who carried you in their prayers long before you were born. They endured. They worked. They believed. And they passed that strength forward through time, through pain, through silence until it reached me.

Now it's my turn. My honor. My calling. To pass it on to you.

You are never alone. There's a whole tribe behind you.

I catch myself saying things now that my parents used to tell me. Even thinking the way they thought. It makes me smile. Legacy isn't just what we leave behind. It's how we live on in each other.

And if you remember anything from me, let it be this: Time is precious. It's the only thing you can't get back. Faith means not wasting today on yesterday's regrets. It means living now with purpose, with trust, for the tomorrow still ahead.

Faith, Redefined

If you asked me now, after everything I've lived through, "What is faith?" this is what I'd say:

Faith is trust planted deep inside you. Not always loud. Not flashy. But always there.

It's the bridge between what you dream and what you live, between what's possible and where you are right now.

Faith isn't just something you reach for when you're desperate. It's something you grow. Something you pay attention to. Something you use every day.

And when you do use it really lean on it, it has a way of coming back. Filled up again.

By what you've been through. By what you've survived. Even with the pain.

It's not a one-time gift. It's a gift that keeps giving when you keep trusting.

The Music That Speaks

If you remember me for my music, I hope you remember this: I played with a smile even when I was hurting. That every note I wrote carried both joy and pain. Some songs are more than music. They're heirlooms. Earlier, I explained these songs through craft and circumstance. This time, I'm explaining them through love.

Good Morning, Mr. Bruce, was written for the first teacher who believed in me. Remember When We Remembered about memory itself. How fragile it is. How precious. How sacred. When God Hears was written after a long season of feeling unseen, unheard. Wondering if God noticed my prayers spoken or silent, played on keys or held in my heart. Only to learn that He had been listening all along.

I hope you carry these forward not just as recordings, but as treasures. As reminders that music isn't just sound. It's a story. It's survival. It's faith made audible.

Lessons I'd Leave with You

If I could leave you with anything, it would be these truths:

- Faith won't keep you from getting knocked down, but it will help you stand back up.
- Time is the most valuable thing you have. Spend it wisely, guard it fiercely.
- Music is more than entertainment. It is medicine, memory, and message.
- People will fail you, but God's blanket of covering will not.

When I was young, my dad had a phrase he said more times than I can count: "Hey, cat, take care of your mom."

He said it so much it became part of the beat of my life. Sometimes I nodded. Sometimes I rolled my eyes. Sometimes I brushed it off like kids do when they've heard something too often. But when he passed, those words came back loud. Heavy. Clear.

Take care of your mom. It wasn't just a request. It was a legacy. His way of saying: Carry what matters. Protect what you love. Guard what God has given you.

I've tried to live that out. Not perfectly. Not always well. But as best as I could.

Now, when I look at my children and grandchildren, I want to pass on something like it, not the exact words, but the same weight.

Take care of each other. Take care of the name you carry. Take care of the time you've been given.

Because legacy isn't about buildings. Or money. Or how many people know your name?

Legacy is about covering and being someone's shade in the heat. Someone's blanket in the cold.

A Benediction

If this memoir means anything, I hope it shows this: Faith can take a punch hard, and you can still get back up.

I'm not perfect. I'm not unscarred. But I'm here. Still standing.

And if you ever feel sucker punched by life, by loss, by doubt, I want you to remember:
You're not alone. And you're not done.

The same God who covered me on that hill, through hospital rooms, through crashes, through Japan, through long nights on dialysis, He's got a blanket big enough to cover you, too.

So keep walking. Use your time well. Live your faith, even when it's weak. And when life goes quiet, when the music stops, don't wait. Start singing. Write your own song.

FINAL CHAPTER

Still Standing

I f you've made it this far with me, I want to speak plain, not as an author, not as a musician, not as a patient, but as one person to another.

My life has been a long line of sucker punches. Some I've told you about. Others I still carry in silence. But the point isn't how many times I fell. It's that I'm still here. Still standing. And if you're reading this, maybe you are too.

When I was a boy, my grandmother on my dad's side showed me the cross on the hill. Chipped. Weathered. Nothing special to most. But to me, it became a signpost. A quiet reminder that faith, even when fragile, can stand taller than we think.

Then there was my mother's mom, the one who called me "Preacher." She told me God had a big blanket. When it was time for His children to rest, He'd pull it over the sky. For years, I believed it literally. Now I think about it deeply in a different way. That blanket covered me through dialysis

137

nights. Hospital rooms. Airports halfway across the world. Even now, I feel it.

I've carried other voices too. Like Michael in Japan. Not a churchgoer. Not someone who claimed faith. A man tied to the edges of life, part of the Yakuza. But when he saw me afraid before a flight to South Korea, he looked at me and said, "God's got you, Bishop." Of all the sermons I've ever heard, that one sentence stayed the longest. Years later, when I learned he died young just like he said he would, I remembered those words. And I realized: God uses unlikely messengers. Even an atheist can speak the truth that carries weight.

And then there's the music. It's been my other voice. My other prayer.

Good morning, Mr. Bruce. I wrote it for my first piano teacher. A thank-you. A memorial. A way to honor the man who taught me discipline and respect.

Remember When We Remembered was born out of grief, a way to gather broken pieces and turn them into a melody.

And Michael Jackson's "Man in the Mirror" that song still speaks to me. I used to ask God to change everything around me. That chorus reminded me: start with the man in the mirror. Real change begins inside.

Then came When God Hears. That one wasn't written right away. It came after seasons of feeling unheard. Wondering if my prayers, spoken or silent, played or held in my heart, were reaching anyone. Then, slowly, I realized: He was listening all along. The song became that moment of arrival. Breakthrough. Realization. And the feeling, oh, what a feeling it was of knowing you're finally heard.

Now, as a father and grandfather, I hear my parents. My grandparents. In my own voice. I repeat my dad's words: "Take care of your mom." I remember my mom singing in the kitchen. And when I look at my grandchildren, I see them watching me, not yet fully understanding, but sensing something tangible in the way I carry myself. I hope they know this: the faith I've held onto? It's already holding them.

I won't tell you faith kept me from falling. It didn't. I've been on the ground more times than I can count. But faith is why I got back up, why I'm sitting here now, writing these words scarred, yes, but alive.

So if you've ever felt sucker punched in your faith…If you've ever wondered why God seemed silent…If you've ever thought you were the only one getting knocked down…

Let me say this: You are not alone.

Faith doesn't promise you won't get hit. It promises that even after the most brutal blow, you can rise.

Not perfect. Not unscarred. But alive. Faithful. Still standing.

EPILOGUE

The Faith That Remains

*Mama always found a way to make me laugh, even
when I thought I was too grown for her kisses!*

Even after writing those words about standing, about
faith, about finding strength in the storm, life came with
one more blow I wasn't ready for the kind that takes your

breath, your footing, and your sense of time all at once. When my mother passed, faith didn't come wrapped in scriptures or songs. It came in silence. In the soft hum of hospital machines, in the stillness of an empty chair, in the sound of my own heartbeat trying to catch up with what just happened. I didn't feel strong. I didn't feel prepared. I just felt… undone. And yet, even there, something sacred stayed not loud, not sure, but steady. The kind of faith that doesn't lift you out of pain, but holds you inside it until you can breathe again.

There were days I didn't want to talk to God, not out of anger, but out of exhaustion. I'd spent a lifetime fighting to hold onto faith through illness, disappointment, and fear, but this was different. This was personal in a way nothing else had been. The woman who prayed for me through every hard season wasn't here anymore. And I found myself wondering, how do you stand when the one who taught you to stand is gone?

That question became more than words. It became this moment!

For a while, I didn't have an answer. I moved through days on autopilot, doing the things that needed to be done, signing papers, making calls, thanking people whose words I couldn't remember ten minutes later. Nights were harder. That's when her voice would echo not in sound, but in memory. A hum in the kitchen. A laugh that still lived somewhere between my ribs. I started to realize that maybe faith doesn't end with the person who leaves. Perhaps it shifts, changes form, and finds new ways to speak through those who stay.

There's a part of me that still reaches for the phone sometimes. To tell her good news. To hear her say, "I'm proud of you, son." But then I remember the faith she planted wasn't meant to stay in her care forever. It was meant to grow roots in me. And though the ground still feels shaky, I can feel those roots holding.

After she passed, I found an old card Momma left me, which has become a confirmation. A handwritten note that proved what love looks like when words become deeds.

Her handwriting. Her confirmation. My promise kept!

I kept that card close. Not because I needed proof, but because her words carried peace. It felt like both Momma and Daddy were saying, "You did what we asked." *You can rest now.*

And for the first time since she passed, I'm now learning to breathe without breaking.

So no, I don't have all the answers. I still question, I still cry, I still feel the sting of loss in quiet moments. But I also know this: the same God who sat with me through dialysis nights, through broken dreams, through the long road back to belief, He's still here,not explaining. Not fixing and just being.

And somehow, that's enough for today.

Still standing!

There are still mornings I wake up expecting to hear her voice, and nights when the silence feels heavier than I can lift. But maybe faith isn't about lifting the silence, perhaps it's about learning to live inside it without losing hope. My mother used to hum when she cooked gospel songs, old hymns, sometimes just a melody she made up on the spot.

I catch myself doing the same now without even thinking, and that's when I realize she never really left. Her faith still hums through my hands, through the music, through the quiet moments when words won't come. She always said, "God never leaves you where He found you." I used to think that meant things would get easier. Now I think it means He keeps moving us through joy, through sorrow, through the spaces in between, until we see Him more clearly than we did before. I don't stand today because I'm unbreakable. I stand because love didn't end, and faith didn't quit. It just changed shape. And though I still feel the ache of what's gone, I also think the quiet truth of what remains: I'm still standing.

For my mother, whose strength taught me how to rise again and then again.

I'll Always Love You, Momma!

www.ingramcontent.com/pod-product-compliance
Lightning Source LLC
Chambersburg PA
CBHW021155130626
46554CB00005B/1833